ROYAL NAVY
Recruiting (RT) Test

Mike and Dave's

ACKNOWLEDGEMENTS

Chris Tyreman would like to thank Mike Carpenter and Dave Joyner for their support and input with this book.

DISCLAIMER

The authors have made every effort to ensure that the information in this book is correct at the time of writing. However, they cannot assume any responsibility for any errors or omissions and herby disclaim any liability for loss, damage, or disruption resulting from such.

CONTENTS

PHOTOCOPIABLE ANSWER RECORD SHEETS
(CIRCLE OR <u>UNDERLINE</u> YOUR ANSWER)

The following answer record sheets will photocopy perfectly on A4 paper. Alternatively, you can make your own sheets or mark the answers in the book.

Answer Record Sheet: TEST 1

Reasoning

RQ1	A	B	C	D	E
RQ2	A	B	C	D	E
RQ3	A	B	C	D	E
RQ4	A	B	C	D	E
RQ5	A	B	C	D	E
RQ6	A	B	C	D	E
RQ7	A	B	C	D	E
RQ8	A	B	C	D	E
RQ9	A	B	C	D	E
RQ10	A	B	C	D	E
RQ11	A	B	C	D	E
RQ12	A	B	C	D	E
RQ13	A	B	C	D	E
RQ14	A	B	C	D	E
RQ15	A	B	C	D	E
RQ16	A	B	C	D	E
RQ17	A	B	C	D	E
RQ18	A	B	C	D	E
RQ19	A	B	C	D	E
RQ20	A	B	C	D	E
RQ21	A	B	C	D	E
RQ22	A	B	C	D	E
RQ23	A	B	C	D	E
RQ24	A	B	C	D	E
RQ25	A	B	C	D	E
RQ26	A	B	C	D	E
RQ27	A	B	C	D	E
RQ28	A	B	C	D	E
RQ29	A	B	C	D	E
RQ30	A	B	C	D	E

Verbal Ability

VQ1	A	B	C	D	E
VQ2	A	B	C	D	E
VQ3	A	B	C	D	E
VQ4	A	B	C	D	E
VQ5	A	B	C	D	E
VQ6	A	B	C	D	E
VQ7	A	B	C	D	E
VQ8	A	B	C	D	E
VQ9	A	B	C	D	E
VQ10	A	B	C	D	E
VQ11	A	B	C	D	E
VQ12	A	B	C	D	E
VQ13	A	B	C	D	E
VQ14	A	B	C	D	E
VQ15	A	B	C	D	E
VQ16	A	B	C	D	E
VQ17	A	B	C	D	E
VQ18	A	B	C	D	E
VQ19	A	B	C	D	E
VQ20	A	B	C	D	E
VQ21	A	B	C	D	E
VQ22	A	B	C	D	E
VQ23	A	B	C	D	E
VQ24	A	B	C	D	E
VQ25	A	B	C	D	E
VQ26	A	B	C	D	E
VQ27	A	B	C	D	E
VQ28	A	B	C	D	E
VQ29	A	B	C	D	E
VQ30	A	B	C	D	E

Answer Record Sheet: TEST 1

Numerical Reasoning

NQ1	A	B	C	D	E
NQ2	A	B	C	D	E
NQ3	A	B	C	D	E
NQ4	A	B	C	D	E
NQ5	A	B	C	D	E
NQ6	A	B	C	D	E
NQ7	A	B	C	D	E
NQ8	A	B	C	D	E
NQ9	A	B	C	D	E
NQ10	A	B	C	D	E
NQ11	A	B	C	D	E
NQ12	A	B	C	D	E
NQ13	A	B	C	D	E
NQ14	A	B	C	D	E
NQ15	A	B	C	D	E
NQ16	A	B	C	D	E
NQ17	A	B	C	D	E
NQ18	A	B	C	D	E
NQ19	A	B	C	D	E
NQ20	A	B	C	D	E
NQ21	A	B	C	D	E
NQ22	A	B	C	D	E
NQ23	A	B	C	D	E
NQ24	A	B	C	D	E
NQ25	A	B	C	D	E
NQ26	A	B	C	D	E
NQ27	A	B	C	D	E
NQ28	A	B	C	D	E
NQ29	A	B	C	D	E
NQ30	A	B	C	D	E

Mechanical Comprehension

MQ1	A	B	C	D
MQ2	A	B	C	D
MQ3	A	B	C	D
MQ4	A	B	C	D
MQ5	A	B	C	D
MQ6	A	B	C	D
MQ7	A	B	C	D
MQ8	A	B	C	D
MQ9	A	B	C	D
MQ10	A	B	C	D
MQ11	A	B	C	D
MQ12	A	B	C	D
MQ13	A	B	C	D
MQ14	A	B	C	D
MQ15	A	B	C	D
MQ16	A	B	C	D
MQ17	A	B	C	D
MQ18	A	B	C	D
MQ19	A	B	C	D
MQ20	A	B	C	D
MQ21	A	B	C	D
MQ22	A	B	C	D
MQ23	A	B	C	D
MQ24	A	B	C	D
MQ25	A	B	C	D
MQ26	A	B	C	D
MQ27	A	B	C	D
MQ28	A	B	C	D
MQ29	A	B	C	D
MQ30	A	B	C	D

Answer Record Sheet: TEST 2

Reasoning

RQ1	A	B	C	D	E
RQ2	A	B	C	D	E
RQ3	A	B	C	D	E
RQ4	A	B	C	D	E
RQ5	A	B	C	D	E
RQ6	A	B	C	D	E
RQ7	A	B	C	D	E
RQ8	A	B	C	D	E
RQ9	A	B	C	D	E
RQ10	A	B	C	D	E
RQ11	A	B	C	D	E
RQ12	A	B	C	D	E
RQ13	A	B	C	D	E
RQ14	A	B	C	D	E
RQ15	A	B	C	D	E
RQ16	A	B	C	D	E
RQ17	A	B	C	D	E
RQ18	A	B	C	D	E
RQ19	A	B	C	D	E
RQ20	A	B	C	D	E
RQ21	A	B	C	D	E
RQ22	A	B	C	D	E
RQ23	A	B	C	D	E
RQ24	A	B	C	D	E
RQ25	A	B	C	D	E
RQ26	A	B	C	D	E
RQ27	A	B	C	D	E
RQ28	A	B	C	D	E
RQ29	A	B	C	D	E
RQ30	A	B	C	D	E

Verbal Ability

VQ1	A	B	C	D	E
VQ2	A	B	C	D	E
VQ3	A	B	C	D	E
VQ4	A	B	C	D	E
VQ5	A	B	C	D	E
VQ6	A	B	C	D	E
VQ7	A	B	C	D	E
VQ8	A	B	C	D	E
VQ9	A	B	C	D	E
VQ10	A	B	C	D	E
VQ11	A	B	C	D	E
VQ12	A	B	C	D	E
VQ13	A	B	C	D	E
VQ14	A	B	C	D	E
VQ15	A	B	C	D	E
VQ16	A	B	C	D	E
VQ17	A	B	C	D	E
VQ18	A	B	C	D	E
VQ19	A	B	C	D	E
VQ20	A	B	C	D	E
VQ21	A	B	C	D	E
VQ22	A	B	C	D	E
VQ23	A	B	C	D	E
VQ24	A	B	C	D	E
VQ25	A	B	C	D	E
VQ26	A	B	C	D	E
VQ27	A	B	C	D	E
VQ28	A	B	C	D	E
VQ29	A	B	C	D	E
VQ30	A	B	C	D	E

Answer Record Sheet: TEST 2

Numerical Reasoning

NQ1	A	B	C	D	E
NQ2	A	B	C	D	E
NQ3	A	B	C	D	E
NQ4	A	B	C	D	E
NQ5	A	B	C	D	E
NQ6	A	B	C	D	E
NQ7	A	B	C	D	E
NQ8	A	B	C	D	E
NQ9	A	B	C	D	E
NQ10	A	B	C	D	E
NQ11	A	B	C	D	E
NQ12	A	B	C	D	E
NQ13	A	B	C	D	E
NQ14	A	B	C	D	E
NQ15	A	B	C	D	E
NQ16	A	B	C	D	E
NQ17	A	B	C	D	E
NQ18	A	B	C	D	E
NQ19	A	B	C	D	E
NQ20	A	B	C	D	E
NQ21	A	B	C	D	E
NQ22	A	B	C	D	E
NQ23	A	B	C	D	E
NQ24	A	B	C	D	E
NQ25	A	B	C	D	E
NQ26	A	B	C	D	E
NQ27	A	B	C	D	E
NQ28	A	B	C	D	E
NQ29	A	B	C	D	E
NQ30	A	B	C	D	E

Mechanical Comprehension

MQ1	A	B	C	D
MQ2	A	B	C	D
MQ3	A	B	C	D
MQ4	A	B	C	D
MQ5	A	B	C	D
MQ6	A	B	C	D
MQ7	A	B	C	D
MQ8	A	B	C	D
MQ9	A	B	C	D
MQ10	A	B	C	D
MQ11	A	B	C	D
MQ12	A	B	C	D
MQ13	A	B	C	D
MQ14	A	B	C	D
MQ15	A	B	C	D
MQ16	A	B	C	D
MQ17	A	B	C	D
MQ18	A	B	C	D
MQ19	A	B	C	D
MQ20	A	B	C	D
MQ21	A	B	C	D
MQ22	A	B	C	D
MQ23	A	B	C	D
MQ24	A	B	C	D
MQ25	A	B	C	D
MQ26	A	B	C	D
MQ27	A	B	C	D
MQ28	A	B	C	D
MQ29	A	B	C	D
MQ30	A	B	C	D

Answer Record Sheet: TEST 3

Reasoning

RQ1	A	B	C	D	E
RQ2	A	B	C	D	E
RQ3	A	B	C	D	E
RQ4	A	B	C	D	E
RQ5	A	B	C	D	E
RQ6	A	B	C	D	E
RQ7	A	B	C	D	E
RQ8	A	B	C	D	E
RQ9	A	B	C	D	E
RQ10	A	B	C	D	E
RQ11	A	B	C	D	E
RQ12	A	B	C	D	E
RQ13	A	B	C	D	E
RQ14	A	B	C	D	E
RQ15	A	B	C	D	E
RQ16	A	B	C	D	E
RQ17	A	B	C	D	E
RQ18	A	B	C	D	E
RQ19	A	B	C	D	E
RQ20	A	B	C	D	E
RQ21	A	B	C	D	E
RQ22	A	B	C	D	E
RQ23	A	B	C	D	E
RQ24	A	B	C	D	E
RQ25	A	B	C	D	E
RQ26	A	B	C	D	E
RQ27	A	B	C	D	E
RQ28	A	B	C	D	E
RQ29	A	B	C	D	E
RQ30	A	B	C	D	E

Verbal Ability

VQ1	A	B	C	D	E
VQ2	A	B	C	D	E
VQ3	A	B	C	D	E
VQ4	A	B	C	D	E
VQ5	A	B	C	D	E
VQ6	A	B	C	D	E
VQ7	A	B	C	D	E
VQ8	A	B	C	D	E
VQ9	A	B	C	D	E
VQ10	A	B	C	D	E
VQ11	A	B	C	D	E
VQ12	A	B	C	D	E
VQ13	A	B	C	D	E
VQ14	A	B	C	D	E
VQ15	A	B	C	D	E
VQ16	A	B	C	D	E
VQ17	A	B	C	D	E
VQ18	A	B	C	D	E
VQ19	A	B	C	D	E
VQ20	A	B	C	D	E
VQ21	A	B	C	D	E
VQ22	A	B	C	D	E
VQ23	A	B	C	D	E
VQ24	A	B	C	D	E
VQ25	A	B	C	D	E
VQ26	A	B	C	D	E
VQ27	A	B	C	D	E
VQ28	A	B	C	D	E
VQ29	A	B	C	D	E
VQ30	A	B	C	D	E

Answer Record Sheet: TEST 3

Numerical Reasoning						Mechanical Comprehension				
NQ1	A	B	C	D	E	MQ1	A	B	C	D
NQ2	A	B	C	D	E	MQ2	A	B	C	D
NQ3	A	B	C	D	E	MQ3	A	B	C	D
NQ4	A	B	C	D	E	MQ4	A	B	C	D
NQ5	A	B	C	D	E	MQ5	A	B	C	D
NQ6	A	B	C	D	E	MQ6	A	B	C	D
NQ7	A	B	C	D	E	MQ7	A	B	C	D
NQ8	A	B	C	D	E	MQ8	A	B	C	D
NQ9	A	B	C	D	E	MQ9	A	B	C	D
NQ10	A	B	C	D	E	MQ10	A	B	C	D
NQ11	A	B	C	D	E	MQ11	A	B	C	D
NQ12	A	B	C	D	E	MQ12	A	B	C	D
NQ13	A	B	C	D	E	MQ13	A	B	C	D
NQ14	A	B	C	D	E	MQ14	A	B	C	D
NQ15	A	B	C	D	E	MQ15	A	B	C	D
NQ16	A	B	C	D	E	MQ16	A	B	C	D
NQ17	A	B	C	D	E	MQ17	A	B	C	D
NQ18	A	B	C	D	E	MQ18	A	B	C	D
NQ19	A	B	C	D	E	MQ19	A	B	C	D
NQ20	A	B	C	D	E	MQ20	A	B	C	D
NQ21	A	B	C	D	E	MQ21	A	B	C	D
NQ22	A	B	C	D	E	MQ22	A	B	C	D
NQ23	A	B	C	D	E	MQ23	A	B	C	D
NQ24	A	B	C	D	E	MQ24	A	B	C	D
NQ25	A	B	C	D	E	MQ25	A	B	C	D
NQ26	A	B	C	D	E	MQ26	A	B	C	D
NQ27	A	B	C	D	E	MQ27	A	B	C	D
NQ28	A	B	C	D	E	MQ28	A	B	C	D
NQ29	A	B	C	D	E	MQ29	A	B	C	D
NQ30	A	B	C	D	E	MQ30	A	B	C	D

Answer Record Sheet: TEST 4

Reasoning						Verbal Ability					
RQ1	A	B	C	D	E	VQ1	A	B	C	D	E
RQ2	A	B	C	D	E	VQ2	A	B	C	D	E
RQ3	A	B	C	D	E	VQ3	A	B	C	D	E
RQ4	A	B	C	D	E	VQ4	A	B	C	D	E
RQ5	A	B	C	D	E	VQ5	A	B	C	D	E
RQ6	A	B	C	D	E	VQ6	A	B	C	D	E
RQ7	A	B	C	D	E	VQ7	A	B	C	D	E
RQ8	A	B	C	D	E	VQ8	A	B	C	D	E
RQ9	A	B	C	D	E	VQ9	A	B	C	D	E
RQ10	A	B	C	D	E	VQ10	A	B	C	D	E
RQ11	A	B	C	D	E	VQ11	A	B	C	D	E
RQ12	A	B	C	D	E	VQ12	A	B	C	D	E
RQ13	A	B	C	D	E	VQ13	A	B	C	D	E
RQ14	A	B	C	D	E	VQ14	A	B	C	D	E
RQ15	A	B	C	D	E	VQ15	A	B	C	D	E
RQ16	A	B	C	D	E	VQ16	A	B	C	D	E
RQ17	A	B	C	D	E	VQ17	A	B	C	D	E
RQ18	A	B	C	D	E	VQ18	A	B	C	D	E
RQ19	A	B	C	D	E	VQ19	A	B	C	D	E
RQ20	A	B	C	D	E	VQ20	A	B	C	D	E
RQ21	A	B	C	D	E	VQ21	A	B	C	D	E
RQ22	A	B	C	D	E	VQ22	A	B	C	D	E
RQ23	A	B	C	D	E	VQ23	A	B	C	D	E
RQ24	A	B	C	D	E	VQ24	A	B	C	D	E
RQ25	A	B	C	D	E	VQ25	A	B	C	D	E
RQ26	A	B	C	D	E	VQ26	A	B	C	D	E
RQ27	A	B	C	D	E	VQ27	A	B	C	D	E
RQ28	A	B	C	D	E	VQ28	A	B	C	D	E
RQ29	A	B	C	D	E	VQ29	A	B	C	D	E
RQ30	A	B	C	D	E	VQ30	A	B	C	D	E

Answer Record Sheet: TEST 4

Numerical Reasoning						Mechanical Comprehension				
NQ1	A	B	C	D	E	MQ1	A	B	C	D
NQ2	A	B	C	D	E	MQ2	A	B	C	D
NQ3	A	B	C	D	E	MQ3	A	B	C	D
NQ4	A	B	C	D	E	MQ4	A	B	C	D
NQ5	A	B	C	D	E	MQ5	A	B	C	D
NQ6	A	B	C	D	E	MQ6	A	B	C	D
NQ7	A	B	C	D	E	MQ7	A	B	C	D
NQ8	A	B	C	D	E	MQ8	A	B	C	D
NQ9	A	B	C	D	E	MQ9	A	B	C	D
NQ10	A	B	C	D	E	MQ10	A	B	C	D
NQ11	A	B	C	D	E	MQ11	A	B	C	D
NQ12	A	B	C	D	E	MQ12	A	B	C	D
NQ13	A	B	C	D	E	MQ13	A	B	C	D
NQ14	A	B	C	D	E	MQ14	A	B	C	D
NQ15	A	B	C	D	E	MQ15	A	B	C	D
NQ16	A	B	C	D	E	MQ16	A	B	C	D
NQ17	A	B	C	D	E	MQ17	A	B	C	D
NQ18	A	B	C	D	E	MQ18	A	B	C	D
NQ19	A	B	C	D	E	MQ19	A	B	C	D
NQ20	A	B	C	D	E	MQ20	A	B	C	D
NQ21	A	B	C	D	E	MQ21	A	B	C	D
NQ22	A	B	C	D	E	MQ22	A	B	C	D
NQ23	A	B	C	D	E	MQ23	A	B	C	D
NQ24	A	B	C	D	E	MQ24	A	B	C	D
NQ25	A	B	C	D	E	MQ25	A	B	C	D
NQ26	A	B	C	D	E	MQ26	A	B	C	D
NQ27	A	B	C	D	E	MQ27	A	B	C	D
NQ28	A	B	C	D	E	MQ28	A	B	C	D
NQ29	A	B	C	D	E	MQ29	A	B	C	D
NQ30	A	B	C	D	E	MQ30	A	B	C	D

INTRODUCTION

This book comprises a skills review section for each of the four areas of the Royal Navy Recruiting Test, followed by four full practice tests. Together, these provide plenty of tuition and practice for candidates sitting the test. The book does not offer insights into the interview or selection processes for the Navy, because this is not the intention.

The four tests are exactly the same length as the actual test. You should aim to complete each section of the test in the times shown below. However, only the very best candidates are likely to reach the end of each section in these times.

Reasoning test (30 questions in 9 minutes: 18 seconds/question)

Verbal Ability test (30 questions in 9 minutes: 18 seconds/question)

Numerical test (30 questions in 16 minutes: 32 seconds/question)

Mechanical Comprehension test (30 questions in 10 minutes: 20 seconds/question)

Aim to get half the questions correct (50%) in Test 1 in the time available, and three-quarters (75%) correct with extra time. Naturally, your mark will tend to improve as you work through the remaining tests. However, these have been graded slightly, with the most difficult test (Test 4) coming last, so do not expect to see a big improvement in your marks. Make good use of the expanded answers at the back of the book with any wrong answers, so that you can be clear on where you went wrong and what you need to revise.

Good luck

Mike and Dave

ROYAL NAVY
RECRUITING (RT) TEST
MECHANICAL COMPREHENSION
SKILLS REVIEW

1. Levers, force, mechanical advantage and energy

Over 2000 years ago, the Greek mathematician, Archimedes, said "Give me a lever long enough and a fulcrum on which to place it, and I shall move the world". Any weight can be lifted if the lever is long enough to do it.

The easiest lever to understand is the Class 1 lever, where the load (weight) and the force (effort) required to lift it are on either side of the *fulcrum* or pivot, similar to a seesaw. The lighter person sits farther away from to the pivot to create a longer lever arm. A person half as heavy needs to sit twice as far from the pivot to balance a person of double the weight.

Balance: weight x distance left side = weight x distance right side

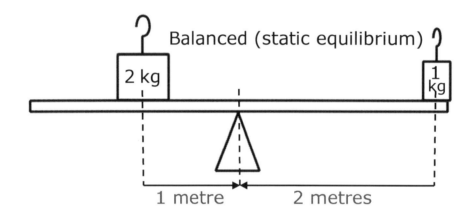

Lever formula where a force or 'effort' is used to balance a load:
effort x lever arm = load x lever arm

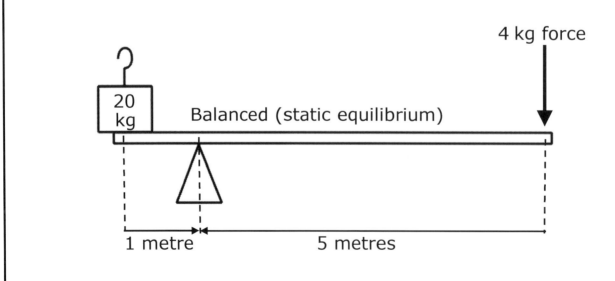

Mechanical advantage (MA) is the ratio of machines output force to its input force.

Mechanical Advantage (MA) formula:
MA = load divided by effort   (or force out ÷ force in)

A lever is a simple machine that allows a heavier weight to be lifted by a smaller force. The MA of a lever can be calculated from the ratio of the input arm length to the output arm length.

Mechanical Advantage (MA) formula for a lever:
MA = input arm length divided by output arm length

The lever shown below has a mechanical advantage (MA) of 5. It might appear that the lever gives you 'something for nothing' because the weight can be lifted by a force five-times smaller. However, the force (F) moves five times farther more than load (W) lifts.

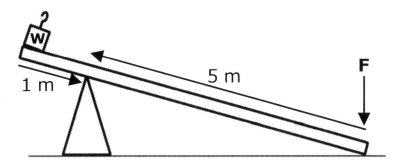

So the MA is also the ratio of the distances moved (movement ratio). To help with the understanding of levers (and other simple machines), it is worth remembering that levers do not create energy, as this would be impossible. The energy used to lift a load a given distance is the same whether a lever is used or not. Energy is the effort of doing work and can be calculated as follows:

Energy (joules, J) = work done = force (newton, N) x distance (m)
(There are 10 newtons per kilogram)

It takes the same amount of energy (100 J) to move a 1 kilogram load through 10 metres as it does to move a 10 kg load through 1 metre. You move a small force a long distance with a lever and the payoff is a large force or weight moving a shorter distance.

2. Pulleys ('block and tackle' systems)

These machines permit heavy loads to be lifted by hand using a series of pulleys that split the load between a number of moving ropes. As with levers, the load is moved a shorter distance than the 'effort' which is applied to do it. A pulley that lifts a load of 100 kg a height of 1 metre with a effort of 25 kg has a mechanical advantage of 4; the rope has to be pulled four times farther, or 4 metres, to balance the work done in lifting the load 1 metre. In any question about pulleys (and levers) the effect of friction forces and the weight of the pulleys is ignored (100% efficiency is assumed).

There is more than one way to calculate the mechanical advantage (MA) of a system of pulleys. However, to be clear what the effect of mechanical advantage is, below are the forces in kg needed to lift a weight of 100 kg one metre off the ground with the MA shown.

MA	Force (in kg) needed to lift 100 kg	Length of rope pulled(m)
1	100 (100 ÷ 1)	1 m (1m x 1)
2	50 (100 ÷ 2)	2 m (1m x 2)
3	33.3 (100 ÷ 3)	3 m (1m x 3)
4	25 (100 ÷ 4)	4 m (1m x 4)
5	20 (100 ÷ 5)	5 m (1m x 5)

When the MA is 1 the force needed to lift the weight is the same as the weight itself and the force moves the same distance as the weight. Where the MA is 2 the force needed to lift the weight is half the weight and the force moves twice as far to lift the load the same distance

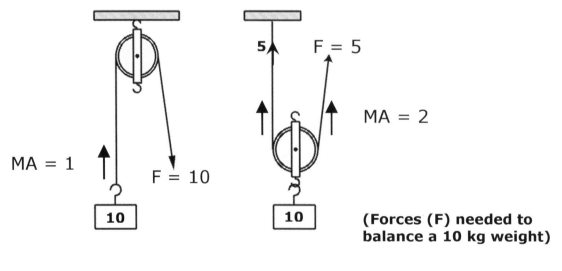

(Forces (F) needed to balance a 10 kg weight)

20

There are two main types of pulley: moving (or 'traveling block') and non-moving. Non-moving pulleys are usually <u>suspended</u> from an overhead support for example a beam or ceiling. These pulleys offer <u>no increase in MA</u> but they do allow the direction of the effort to be changed, so a weight can be lifted by pulling downwards or sideways for example.

Non-moving pulleys system mechanical advantage:
MA = 1 (no reduction in the effort needed to lift the load).

Moving pulleys or 'traveling blocks' are <u>attached to the load</u> and provide an MA of more than 1 because the length of rope drawn out is more than the distance the load moves. There are different methods of working out the MA of pulley systems by counting the number of moving pulleys and ropes. However, one of the easiest methods is to observe the following rules:

Moving pulley system mechanical advantage formula:
MA = number of lengths of rope on each side of the pulley(s) including the free end; subtract 1 if the free end is pulled down towards the load

MA =   2   3   4   5

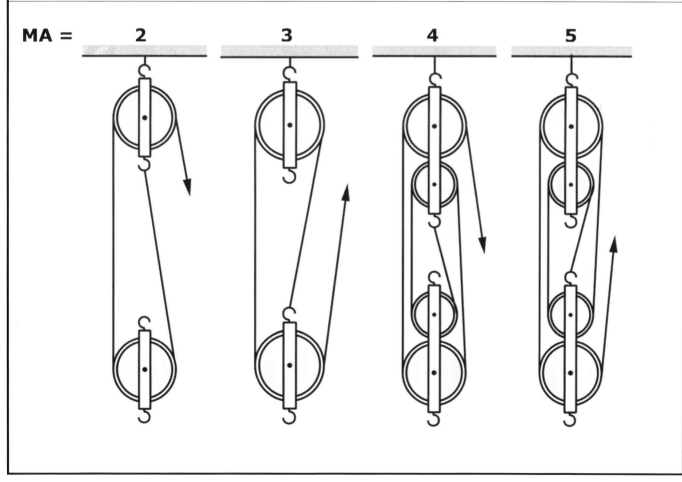

3. Gears, chain drives and belt drives

These questions are concerned with speed and direction of rotation. There are only two directions of rotation to consider – clockwise, in the same direction as the hands move on a clock, and anticlockwise in the opposite direction to the hands on a clock.

Rules of rotation for an interlocking pair of gears:

Gears of equal size must have the same number of teeth to interlock properly.

Interlocking gears turn in opposite directions (clockwise (CW) and anti-clockwise (ACW))

Interlocking gears of the equal size must rotate at the same speed (same revolutions per minute (rpm)).

A larger gear has more teeth and turns the slowest.

A smaller gear has fewer teeth and turns the quickest.

The ratio of teeth determines the relative speeds of the gears; if one gear has half as may teeth as the other gear then it turns at twice the speed; a gear with 8 teeth turns at twice the speed of a gear with 16.

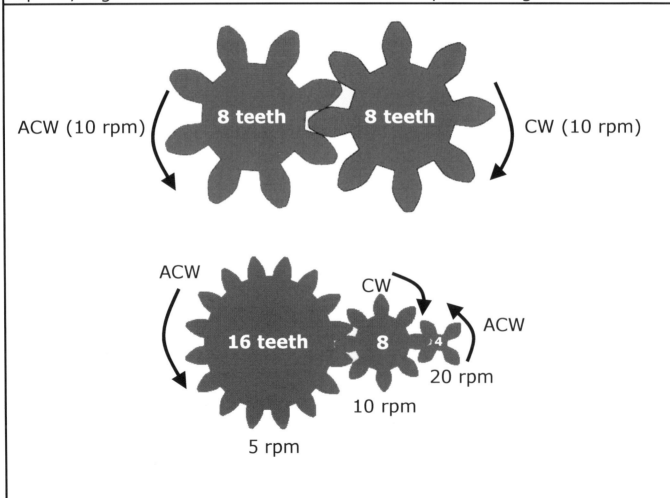

Rules for gears in series (on different axles):

With an even number of gears (2, 4, 6, 8, 10 etc), the first and last gears always turn in opposite directions.

With an odd number of gears (3, 5, 7, 9, 11 etc), the first and last gears always turn in the same directions.

The first and last gears in any system of multiple gears always turn at the same speed if they have the same number of gears (however many interlocking gears there are between them and whatever number of teeth the other gears have).

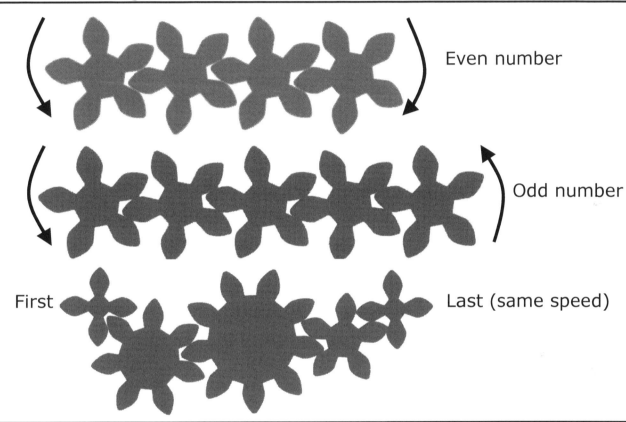

Even number

Odd number

First   Last (same speed)

Rules for multiple gears on the same axle (compound system):

All gears on the same axle must rotate at the same speed and in the same direction (the gears are fixed together); e.g. as per gearboxes.

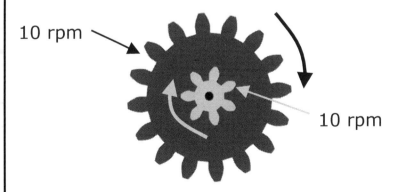

10 rpm

10 rpm

Rules for gears driven by a chain (e.g. bicycle gears):

Where gears are driven by a chain, the direction of the chain determines the direction of rotation of all the gears. Gears inside the chain will rotate in the same direction as the chain. Gears outside the chain are driven in the opposite direction to the chain.

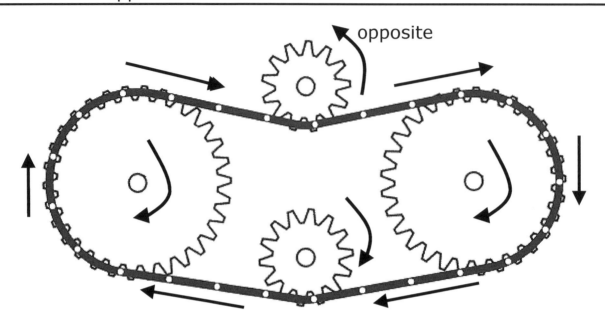

Rules for belt driven gears, wheels and drums

The direction of rotation of the belt determines the direction of rotation of the rollers.

If the belt crosses-over the direction of rotation is reversed.

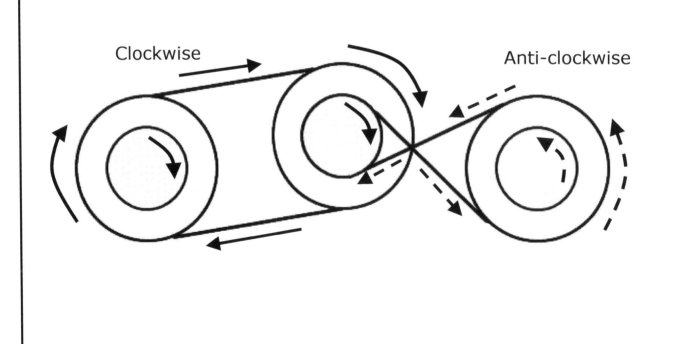

4. Springs and Hooke's law

In the 17th century the physicist Robert Hooke showed that the stretch of a coil spring (extension) is directly proportional (linear) to the force or load it supports. So for example, a spring supporting a 2 kg load will stretch twice as much as a spring supporting a 1 kg load. This law also applies to the compression of a spring, as in a car suspension. Whilst the behaviour of a coil spring seems obvious, most questions include more than one spring to make things more complicated.

Rules of extension/compression for two (or more) coil springs:

When two springs are placed in parallel (side by side) the load is SPLIT between them and the stretch (or compression) is HALF what it would have been with one spring on its own.

When two springs are joined in series (e.g. one above the other) the load is carried by BOTH springs (not split) and the stretch (or compression) is DOUBLE what is would have been with one spring on its own.

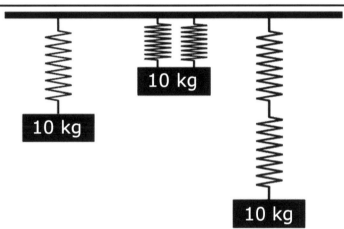

5. Pressure and buoyancy.

Pressure is force divided by area. So for example, the stiletto heel of a shoe generates more pressure than an elephants foot, despite the massive weight of the elephant. The Imperial units of pressure are pounds per square inch (psi) and the metric units are Newtons per metre squared (N/m^2), also known as Pascals (Pa).

Pressure (P) = Force (F) ÷ Area (A)

Multiplying both sides of the equation by 'Area' gives:
Pressure (P) x Area (A) = Force (F)

This means that for a given pressure the force increases with increasing area, which is the principle behind the hydraulic piston.

The principles of pressure (force divided by area) can be applied to all three physical states, namely gas, liquid and solid. Whilst gases are easily compressed and solids deform or fracture, liquids are incompressible, so their volume remains the same whatever pressure is applied. In contrast, gases shrink in volume when the pressure is increased (or the temperature is lowered) and expand when the pressure is reduced or the temperature increased (as per a hot air balloon).

The hydraulic piston forms the basis of a car's braking system, where the master cylinder, pushed by the peddle, transmits force through the brake fluid to operate a slave cylinder at the brake disc.

Hydraulic system piston rule:
The hydraulic pressure in a closed system remains constant so the force is magnified (or reduced) in proportion to the cross-sectional surface areas of the two pistons (the diameters squared). The larger the piston the greater the force generated.

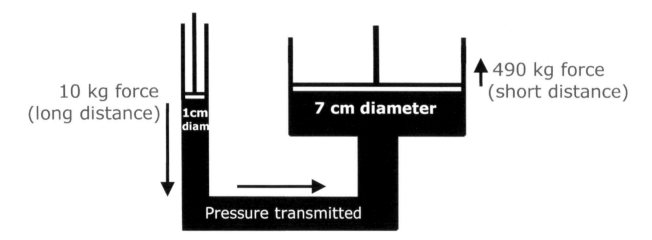

In an open system, the pressure in a liquid is directly proportional to the depth below the surface of the liquid; it is exerted equally in all directions. This is known as hydrostatic pressure (static fluid pressure) and is generated by the weight of the fluid. The hydrostatic pressure in oil is less than in water because oil weighs less (oil is less dense than water).

Hydrostatic pressure rule for a given fluid:
Pressure (P) is proportional to: depth below the surface

A convenient unit of pressure is one atmosphere (1 atm) or 1 bar, which is equivalent to 14.7 psi or 100,000 Pa (100kPa) at sea level. This pressure is determined by the height of a column of air rising up to the edge of the atmosphere. The air pressure on the summit of Everest is only 4.9 psi (one-third of a bar).

For a submarine in the ocean, the pressure on the hull increases above atmospheric pressure in proportion to the depth below the surface. The pressure increases by about 1 bar for every 10 metres of depth.

Depth below sea level	Increase in pressure
10 metres	1 bar
50 metres	50 bar
100 metres	100 bar
500 metres	500 bar

When a submarine sinks it displaces a volume of water exactly equal to its own volume. The weight of this water creates a positive up-thrust or buoyancy force as first described by Archimedes.

Archimedes principle:
The buoyant force experienced by an object immersed in a fluid (e.g. water, oil, air) is equal to the weight of the fluid it displaces.
When a ship floats, the weight of water displaced by the hull exactly matches the weight of the ship.

If you find this principle difficult to understand then think about the overall density of the object (density is the concentration of weight, meaning it is the weight per unit volume). An object less dense than water will float in water and an object more dense than water will sink.

Substance	Density (gram/cm^3)
Water	1.0 (neither floats nor sinks in itself)
Ice	0.9 (floats in water with 90% of the ice submerged)
Cork	0.25 (floats in water with 25% of the cork submerged)
Steel	8.0 (sinks completely in water)

Water pressure increases with depth below the surface:

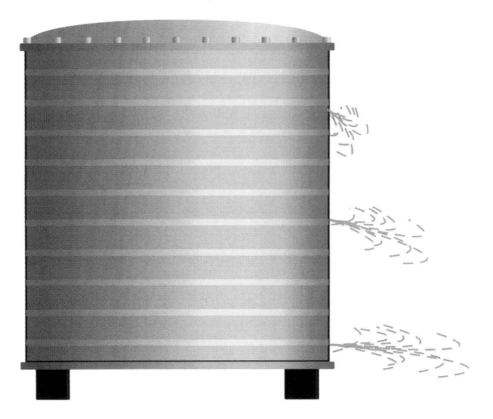

Archimedes: Any floating body displaces its own weight of fluid.

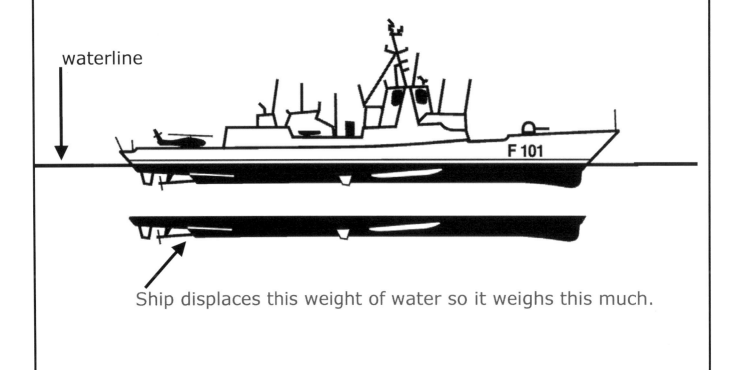

waterline

Ship displaces this weight of water so it weighs this much.

5. Electrical circuits

Questions involving electrical circuits normally involve a power source, a switch and some electrical components. Only a basic knowledge of electricity and electronics is required and some it you will be familiar with already. So for example, a car battery operates at about 12 volts, it has a positive pole and a negative pole; the negative is also known as the earth or ground. Nothing operates until a switch or relay is closed and the wiring must complete a loop from positive to negative via a 'load' that draws current (for example a bulb or resistor).

Electrical components in a circuit are represented by symbols. The most common components are shown below.

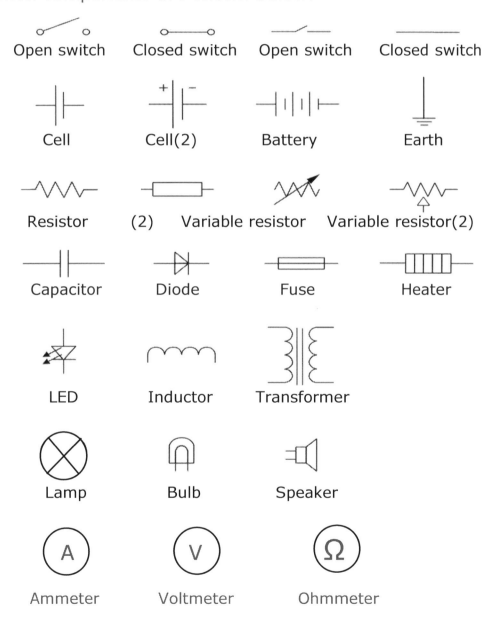

Open switch   Closed switch   Open switch   Closed switch

Cell   Cell(2)   Battery   Earth

Resistor   (2)   Variable resistor   Variable resistor(2)

Capacitor   Diode   Fuse   Heater

LED   Inductor   Transformer

Lamp   Bulb   Speaker

Ammeter   Voltmeter   Ohmmeter

Rules for electrical circuits:

No current flows is there is a break in the wiring to the power source or a switch is left open.

Voltage is an electromotive force that drives current through a component (e.g. a bulb) to make it work.

Voltage (V) is measured across a component whereas current (A) is measured through it.

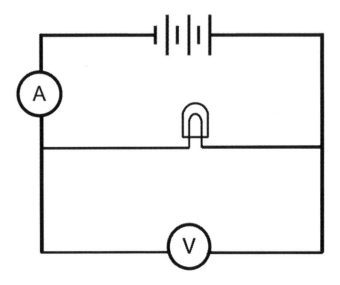

(An ammeter has negligible resistance and causes no 'voltage drop'.)

(A voltmeter has very high resistance and draws negligible current.)

Rules for batteries:

Two identical batteries connected in series (end to end, positive to negative) doubles the voltage.

Two identical batteries connected in parallel (side by side, positive to positive and negative to negative) doubles the current available but the voltage is the same as with one battery.

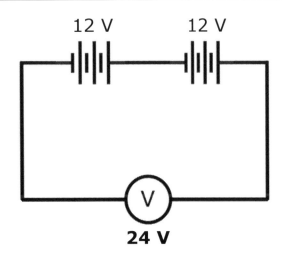

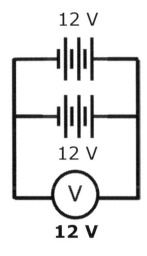

Rules for series circuits (applies to resistors and bulbs):
There is only one pathway for the current to take; adding more resistors or more bulbs reduces the current. Two 10 ohm resistors in a series circuit are equivalent one 20 ohm resistor (the resistance is doubled). The voltage across two resistors or two bulbs is shared between them (the voltage is halved).

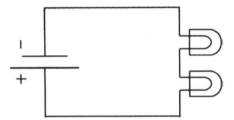

Bulbs connected in <u>series</u> share the battery voltage (half each for identical bulbs); more resistance; current halved; bulbs are dimmed (battery lasts longer).

Rules for parallel circuits (applies to resistors and bulbs):
There is more than one pathway for the current to take; adding more resistors or more bulbs increases the current. Two 10 ohm resistors in a series circuit are equivalent one 5 ohm resistor (resistance is halved). The voltage across any number of resistors or bulbs in a parallel circuit is unchanged (i.e. same as the power source).

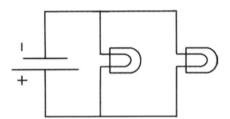

Bulbs connected in <u>parallel</u> both receive the full battery voltage; resistance halved so the current is doubled (twin circuit); both bulbs are fully lit (battery drains quicker).

Rules for combination circuits (series and parallel):
A combination circuit requires three or more resistors (or bulbs), two of which are in parallel with one in series. The two resistors (or bulbs) in parallel combine to give one lesser resistance which is then added to the series resistor to give the total resistance for the circuit.

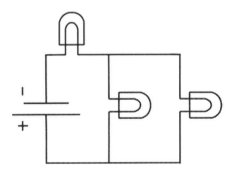

Two bulbs are connected in parallel and one in series with them; total resistance is more than two bulbs in in parallel but less than two bulbs in series. The top bulb is the brightest (but not as bright as two bulbs in parallel nor as dim as two in series).

ROYAL NAVY
RECRUITING (RT) TEST
NUMERICAL REASONING
SKILLS REVIEW

1. Mental arithmetic

Addition
Write down as many steps as you need to in a calculation to avoid making mistakes. Use traditional longhand methods or 'place values' (units, tens, hundreds, thousands) starting with the <u>largest numbers</u>.

Example: 2532 + 1316 is 2000 + 1000 (= 3000)
                                    add on   500 + 300 (= 3800)
                                    add on   32 + 16   (= 3848)

Subtraction
Use traditional longhand methods or 'adding back' techniques.
Example: 756 – 379 is 756 – 400 = 356 (an easy first step) then add back the extra 21 that was taken off in the first step: 356 + 21 = 377

Multiplication
Calculators are not allowed test so memorise the multiplication table.

MULTIPLICATION TABLE

	1	2	3	4	5	6	7	8	9	10	11	12
1	1	2	3	4	5	6	7	8	9	10	11	12
2	2	4	6	8	10	12	14	16	18	21	22	24
3	3	6	9	12	15	18	21	24	27	30	33	36
4	4	8	12	16	20	24	28	32	36	40	44	48
5	5	10	15	20	25	30	35	40	45	50	55	60
6	6	12	18	24	30	36	42	48	54	60	66	72
7	7	14	21	28	35	42	49	56	63	70	77	84
8	8	16	24	32	40	48	56	64	72	80	88	96
9	9	18	27	36	45	54	63	72	81	90	99	108
10	10	20	30	40	50	60	70	80	90	100	110	120
11	11	22	33	44	55	66	77	88	99	110	121	132
12	12	24	36	48	60	72	84	96	108	120	132	144

Example: 7 x 11 = 77

For larger numbers use traditional longhand methods or 'place values'
Example: 1324 x 4 = 4000 + 1200 + 80 + 16 = 5200 + 96 = 5296

Division
Use traditional longhand methods or try scaling numbers up or canceling down (by 2 by 3 by 4 etc) as a first step. For example:
325 ÷ 25 = 1300 ÷ 100 = 13 (scale both numbers up by 4 in a first step so that the 25 becomes 100, which is easy to divide by later).

2. Fractions

Canceling

Fractions are easier to handle when the numbers are small. The top and bottom numbers can sometimes be cancelled by small numbers like 2,3 or 5 to simplify the arithmetic. For example:

$$\frac{18}{24} = \frac{9}{12} = \frac{3}{4}$$ (divide the top and bottom numbers by 2 then by 3)

Rule for the addition or subtraction of fractions

If the bottom numbers are the same, you write the bottom number once and add or subtract the two top numbers. If the bottom numbers are different then you have to 'cross-multiply' first, then put your two answers over the bottom numbers multiplied together.

Same bottom number: $\frac{5}{9} + \frac{2}{9} = \frac{7}{9}$ Similarly: $\frac{5}{9} - \frac{2}{9} = \frac{3}{9} = \frac{1}{3}$

If the bottom numbers are different, then you have a problem, because it is not possible to add, for example, quarters and thirds in a single step. One technique is to 'cross multiply', in a first step so:

$\frac{1}{4} + \frac{2}{3}$ becomes 1x3 plus 2x4, by multiplying diagonal numbers (cross-multiply), to give 3 + 8 = 11, which goes at the top. To find the bottom half of the fraction you multiply the two bottom numbers:

4 x 3 = 12. We then have $\frac{11}{12}$, which is the answer.

Rule for the multiplication of fractions

Multiply the two top numbers together and the two bottom numbers together.

Example: $\frac{5}{9} \times \frac{7}{10} = \frac{5 \times 7}{9 \times 10} = \frac{35}{90} = \frac{7}{18}$ (by dividing the top/bottom by 5); or you can cross-cancel the 5 and the 10 as a first step (before multiplying), to get '1 and 2' so $\frac{5}{9} \times \frac{7}{10}$ becomes: $\frac{1}{9} \times \frac{7}{2} = \frac{7}{18}$

Rule for the division of fraction
This is similar to multiplication except that the fraction on the right-hand side is turned upside down and then multiplied with the fraction on the left-hand side.

Example: $\frac{5}{8} \div \frac{1}{2}$ becomes $\frac{5}{8}$ x $\frac{2}{1}$ = $\frac{10}{8}$ or $1\frac{2}{8}$ (1 whole = $\frac{8}{8}$) = $1\frac{1}{4}$

3. Ratios
These are similar to fractions with the whole divided into a number of parts determined by the ratio.

Rule for working out proportions
Add the ratios together (number of parts), work out the fractions and multiply each fraction by the total you are given.

Example: divide 100 in the ratio 3:2 ('three to two')
1st step: number of parts is 3 + 2 = 5 (five fifths in total)

2nd step: work out the proportional parts (the fractions): $\frac{3}{5}$ and $\frac{2}{5}$

3rd step: multiply the whole by the fractions: $\frac{3}{5}$ x 100 = 3 x 20 = 60;

$\frac{2}{5}$ x 100 = 2 x 20 = 40. Answer: 60 and 40 (100 split 3:2)

4. Decimal numbers
These have decimal point and may/may not include a whole number.

Rule for addition and subtraction of decimals
This is the same as adding ordinary numbers. You retain the place values (tenths, hundredths, thousandths, etc)

Example: 2.000654 + 1.087 + 0.9 = 3.987654

$$
\begin{array}{r}
0.9 \\
1.087 \\
+\ 2.000654 \\
\hline
3.987654
\end{array}
$$

Rule for the multiplication of decimals x 10, x 100, x 1000 etc
When multiplying by 10, 100 or 1000 etc the decimals point is moved to the right by the number of zeros you have.

Example: 0.15 x10 = 1.5   0.15 x100 = 15.0   0.15 x1000 = 150.0

Rule for the multiplication of decimals by any number
Carry out the multiplication ignoring the decimal point and then add it back in using the following rule:

decimals places in the question = decimal places in the answer

Example: 6 x 3.75 = 6 x 375 after ignoring the decimal point
6 x 375 = 6 x 300 + 6 x 70 + 6 x 5 = 1800 + 420 + 30 = 2250
The number of decimal places in the question is 2, so the number in the answer is 2, in which case 2250 becomes 22.50

Example: 2500 x 0.004   Here, instead of ignoring the decimal point we can simply move it (transfer it) to the larger number as a first step, so 2500 x 0.004 becomes 2.500 x 4 = 10

Rule for the division of decimals x 10, x 100, x 1000 etc
This is the reverse of multiplication for multiples (powers) of ten. The decimal point is moved to the left by the number of zeros you have.

20.4 ÷ 10 = 2.04   20.4 ÷ 100 = 0.204   20.4 ÷ 100 = 0204

Division of/by decimal numbers can be done using a multiplication step to make the division easier or by using x10, x100 or x1000 etc. to remove/move the decimal point.

Example 3.45 ÷ 5 = 6.9 ÷ 10 (by doubling both numbers) = 0.69
Alternatively you can using long division methods keeping the decimal point where it is (five into 3 goes 0. then five into 34 goes 6 remainder 4, then five into 45 goes 9 times to give 0.69).

Example: 35 ÷ 0.25   Here we can 'remove' the decimal point by multiplying both numbers by 4, then = 35 ÷ 0.25 = 140 ÷ 1 = 140

5. Fractions to decimals and vice versa

Fraction to decimal

Example 3/8 is re-written as 3.000 (by adding zeros) divided by 8. Now the division is carried out in the usual way:

$$8\,\big|\,\overline{3.^30^60^40} \quad = \quad 0.3\ 7\ 5$$

Decimal to fraction

Here we use 'place values', for example: 0.4 = 4 tenths = 4/10 = 2/5
Similarly 0.04 = 4 hundredths = 4/100 = 1/25

Some decimals and their well known equivalent fractions are shown below:

0.1 = 1/10; 0.125 = 1/8; 0.2 = 1/5; 0.25 = 1/4; 0.375 = 3/8
0.4 = 2/5; 0.5 = 1/2; 0.6 = 3/5; 0.625 = 5/8; 0.75 = 3/4

6. Percentages

These are fractions with bottom numbers of 100. They can also be shown as decimals by moving the decimal point of the top number two places to the left.

Example: $75\% = \dfrac{75}{100} = \dfrac{3}{4}$; or as a decimal $75\% = \dfrac{75.0}{100} = 0.75$

To calculate a percentage of something you multiply the something by the percent expressed either as a fraction or as a decimal.

Example: 40% of 90 = 4/10 x 90 = 4 x 9 = 36; or 40% = 0.4 x 90 = 4 x 9 = 36 (by moving the decimal point to the larger number).

To convert any number to a percent you multiply it 100%
Example 0.4 = 0.4 x 100% = 40%; 2.5 x 100% = 250%;
1/5 x 100% = 100 ÷ 5 = 20%

Percentage change: $= \dfrac{\text{change in value}}{\text{original value}}$ x 100%

Example: a car accelerates from 15 mph to 60 mph? What is the percentage increase in speed?

$$\frac{60-15}{15} \times 100\% = \frac{45}{15} \times 100\% = 3 \times 100\% = 300\% \text{ increase}$$

Example: A car brakes from 60 mph to 15 mph. What is the percentage decrease in speed?

$$\frac{60-15}{60} \times 100\% = \frac{45}{60} \times 100\% = \frac{3}{4} \times 100\% = 75\% \text{ decrease}$$

Always use the original or 'starting value' as the bottom number when calculating percentage change.

7. Rounding numbers

Rules for shortening a number to a _decimal place_ (dp)
If the _number to the right_ of the decimal place you are rounding to is _5 or above_, then you increase the number in the decimal place by 1; if is less than 5 it remains the same.

Example: multiply 2.625 by 5 and give your answer to 2 decimal places (2 dp). Answer 2.625 x 5 = 13.125 = 13.13 to 2 dp.

How to round decimals up or down:
1.1 = 1.0 (to 1 d.p.)
1.2 = 1.0 (to 1 d.p.)
1.3 = 1.0 (to 1 d.p.)
1.4 = 1.0 (to 1 d.p.)
1.5 = 2.0 (to 1 d.p.)
1.6 = 2.0 (to 1 d.p.)
1.7 = 2.0 (to 1 d.p.)
1.8 = 2.0 (to 1 d.p.)
1.9 = 2.0 (to 1 d.p.)
2.0 = 2.0 (to 1 d.p.)

1.910 = 1.91 (to 2 d.p.)
1.940 = 1.94 (to 2 d.p.)
1.945 = 1.95 (to 2 d.p.)
1.950 = 1.95 (to 2 d.p.)
1.955 = 1.96 (to 2 d.p.)
1.995 = 2.00 (to 2 d.p.)

10.49 to the nearest whole number is 10 (round down)
10.50 to the nearest whole number is 11 (round up).

For whole numbers the same rule applies:
1049 to the nearest hundred is 1000
1050 to the nearest hundred is 1100

Rules for shortening a number to a _significant figure_ (sf)

The rules are similar to decimal place in that you look at the number to the right of the significant figure you are rounding to. However, you start from the _left-most non-zero term_ (not from the decimal point). Significant figure can be used with whole numbers as well as decimals.

Example: multiply 2.0625 by 5 and give your answer to 2 significant figures (2 sf). Answer 2.0625 x 5 = $\underline{1}$0.3125 = 10 to 2 sf. Note how you start from the _left-most non-zero term_ (underlined) to find the second significant figure, then round it up or down according to the number after it (the 3).

How to round to significant figures

325715.85 = 300000 to 1 sf
325715.85 = 330000 to 2 sf
325715.85 = 326000 to 3 sf
325715.85 = 325700 to 4 sf
325715.85 = 325720 to 5 sf
325715.85 = 325716 to 6 sf
325715.85 = 325715.9 to 7 sf

0.0032715.85 = 0.003 to 1 sf (and 0.0 to 1 dp)
0.0032715.85 = 0.0033 to 2 sf (and 0.00 to 2 dp)
0.0032715.85 = 0.00327 to 3 sf (and 0.003 to 3 dp)
0.0032715.85 = 0.003272 to 4 sf (and 0.0033 to 4 dp)
0.0032715.85 = 0.0032726 to 5 sf (and 0.00327 to 5 dp)
0.0032715.85 = 0.0032725.9 to 6 sf (and 0.003273 to 6 dp)

Note how the accuracy of the rounding increases with an increasing number of significant figures.

Standard form (scientific notation)

You may not be tested on this topic but it is worth knowing because it is often used in science and engineering.

Example: 129876 in standard form is 1.29876×10^5 Method: use powers of ten so that only <u>1 digit comes in front of a decimal point</u>.

You need to understand 'powers of 10' to be able use standard form.
$10^1 = 10;$ $10^2 = 100;$ $10^3 = 1000;$ $10^4 = 10000;$ $\underline{10^5 = 100000}$
$10^{-1} = 1/10;$ $10^{-2} = 1/100;$ $10^{-3} = 1/1000;$ $10^{-4} = 1/10000$

The following show the correct use of standard form.

$98765.43 = 9.876543 \times 10^4$ in standard form
$0.0001234 = 1.234 \times 10^{-4}$ in standard form

Standard form makes numbers of any size easy to handle.

8. Clocks and time

Analogue/digital clocks

Rules for converting the 12-hour clock to the 24-hour clock
Re-write the 12 hour clock time as a four digit number and add 12 hours to all p.m. times.

Examples: 9.45 am = 0945 (O nine forty-five hours)
9.45 pm = 09.45 + 12 hrs = 2145 (twenty-one forty-five hours)

Fractions of an hour are converted to minutes by multiplying the fraction (or its decimal) by 60 minutes:

¼ hr = 0.25 x 60 = 15 minutes; ½ hr = 0.5 x 60 = 30 minutes

Applicants should recognize the following time conversions:
1 week = 7 days; 1 day = 24 hours; 1 hour = 60 minutes;
1 minute = 60 seconds

Example 2.5 hr ÷ 10 = 0.25 hrs = 0.25 x 60 min = ¼ x 60 = 15 mins

Clock hands questions (tip: wear a wrist watch with hands)

12 hours rotation of the hour hand (small hand) = 360° (full circle)
9 hours rotation of the hour hand (small hand) = 270° (3/4 circle)
8 hours rotation of the hour hand (small hand) = 240° (2/3 circle)
6 hours rotation of the hour hand (small hand) = 180° (1/2 circle)
4 hours rotation of the hour hand (small hand) = 120° (1/3 circle)
3 hours rotation of the hour hand (small hand) = 90° (1/4 circle)
2 hours rotation of the hour hand (small hand) = 60° (1/6 circle)
1 hour rotation of the hour-hand = 360° ÷ 12 = 30° (1/12 circle)
24 hours rotation of the hour hand (small hand) = 720° (2 full circles)

1 hour rotation of the minute hand (large hand) = 360° (full circle)
45 minutes rotation of the minute hand = 270° (3/4 circle)
40 minutes rotation of the minute hand = 240° (2/3 circle)
30 minutes rotation of the minute hand = 180° (1/2 circle)
20 minutes rotation of the minute hand = 120° (1/3 circle)
15 minutes rotation of the minute hand = 90° (1/4 circle)
10 hours rotation of the minute hand = 60° (1/6 circle)
5 minutes rotation of the minute hand = 30° (1/12 circle)
1 minute rotation = 360° ÷ 60 = 6° (1/60 circle)
2 hour rotation of the minute hand = 720° (2 full circles)

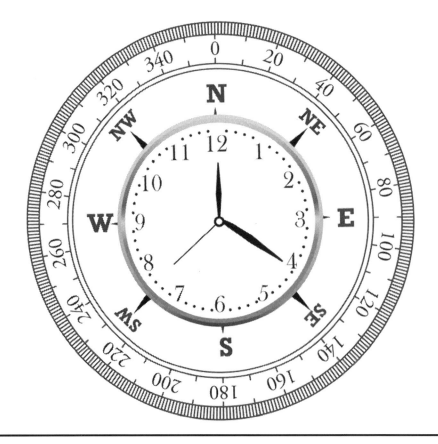

9. Areas, perimeters, volumes and surface area

Rules for areas
Square of side length L = L x L or L^2 (L squared)
Rectangle of base (B) and height (H) = B x H
Triangle: ½ base x vertical height = ½ BH
Circle of radius r: πr^2 (pi r squared; pi = 3.142 or 22/7)
Border region area = area of outer shape – area of inner shape

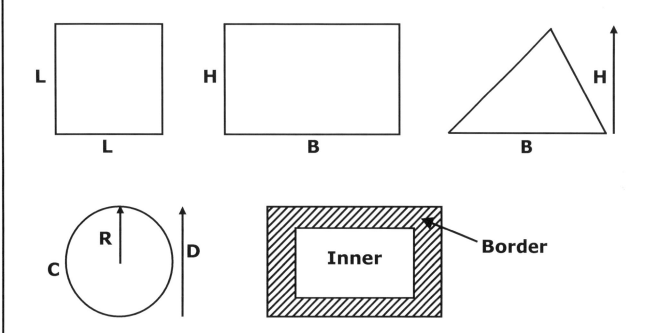

Rules for perimeters
The perimeter is the area all the way around the outside of a shape.
Square = L + L + L + L = 4 x L ('4L')
Rectangle = H + B + H + B = 2H + 2B or 2 x B x H ('2BH')
Circle = circumference (C) = 2 x π x R or $2\pi R$ ('two-pi-R'), and as the diameter (D) is twice the radius (R) then C = π x D or πD ('pi D').

Rules for volumes and surface area of solids
Volume of a cube of side length L = L x L x L = L^3
Volume of a box shape of height H, breadth B and length L = H x B x L
Surface area of a cube = 6 L^2 (total amount of exposed area)
Surface area of a box = 2(BH + LH + BL)

ROYAL NAVY
RECRUITING (RT) TEST
VERBAL ABILITY
SKILLS REVIEW

1.'Word Families'

In these questions one word has a meaning that extends to includes the meaning of all the others. For example: apple, pear, orange and banana can all be classified as fruits.

2. 'Odd one out'

Here you have to choose one word which does not belong with the others. For example: apple, pear, potato, orange and banana. 'Potato' is a vegetable and not a fruit.

3. 'Compound words'

The first word can be joined to the other words to make a new longer word, for example: tea (cup, spoon, pot, break), with one exception (break). We can have a teacup, a teaspoon and a teapot, but not a 'teabreak' because this is two words.

4. 'Make two words'

Similar to 'compound words' except that one word fits in the middle of a pair of words to make two new words. Only one answer will fit both words. For example: day…………..house (time, bird, light, town)
Starting with 'day' we can have 'daytime' and 'daylight' but not 'daybird' and 'daytown', so the answer is either 'time' or 'light' and only light fits with house (lighthouse); daylight and lighthouse.

5. 'Word pair'

Here you have to choose one word that fits the meaning of a pair of words. The pair are typically synonyms. For example:
(fathom and grasp)   seize, measure, understand, depth.
'Fathom and grasp' can both be used to mean 'understand'.

6. 'Missing word'

With these questions you select the missing word that is the best fit in the context of the sentence as a whole. They can test your vocabulary, grammar and spelling skills. For example:
A good interview ……………… is to start off with small talk to put the interviewee at ease: (method   system   technique   practice)
Here the best answer is 'technique' noting that 'method' also fits but it is not the best choice. 'Interview method' (way of doing it) is not as suitable as 'interview technique', which implies method with some skill.

7. 'Related words'

These questions ask you to choose a word that has an opposite meaning or a similar meaning to the word shown. Antonyms are words that have opposite meanings. Examples are:

quick and slow
weak and strong
pass and fail
leave and arrive
exit and entrance
full and empty
large and small
ancient and modern

Synonyms are words that have similar meanings. Examples are:

quick and fast
powerful and strong
truthful and honest
depart and arrive
opening and entrance
full and brimming
big and large
recent and modern

8. 'Analogies'

Here you work out the relationship between one pair of words and use it to identify the missing word. Questions are 'multiple-choice' where the wrong answers that can mislead you. Examples of analogies are:

'kilogram is to weight' as 'metre is to length';
'time is to clock' as 'temperature is to thermometer';
'sun is to moon' as 'day is to night';
'hot is to cold' as 'fast is to slow';
'red is to stop' as 'green is to go';
'walk is to run' (walk faster) as 'leave is to flee' (leave faster).

ROYAL NAVY
RECRUITING (RT) TEST
REASONING
SKILLS REVIEW

1. 'Patterns with numbers'

You can come across several types of number sequence, or number patterns, in the test. Here we cover the main types.

The Arithmetic Progression (A.P.)

In this sequence, the difference between consecutive numbers (or *terms*) remains fixed. The question asks you to find the next number in a sequence.

Example: find the next number in the following sequences:

i) 1, 2, 3, 4, 5, 6, 7, 8, ?   Answer: 9
ii) 3, 5, 7, 9, 11, 13, ?   Answer: 15
iii) 20, 25, 30, 35, 40, ?   Answer: 45
iv) 49, 42, 35, 28, 21, ?   Answer: 14

To find the answer you work out the <u>*common difference*</u> between adjacent numbers then add it to the last number in the sequence. For example, in the third question, the common difference is 5. Adding 5 to each number (or *term*) takes you to the next number: 20 + 5 = 25; 25 + 5 = 30; 30 + 5 = 35; 35 + 5 = 40, so we can predict that the final number is 45 (40 + 5 = 45). In the final example, starting with 49, the numbers become smaller from right to left; the common difference is minus 7 so final number is 21 − 7 = 14

Arithmetic progressions can involve fractions and decimal numbers. Sometimes you are asked to find the missing number rather than the final number. Examples are shown below.

v) $\frac{1}{4}$, $\frac{3}{8}$, ?, $\frac{5}{8}$, $\frac{3}{4}$ Answer: $\frac{1}{2}$ (common difference $= \frac{1}{8}$)

vi) 0.4, 0.9, 1.4, ?, 2.4,   Answer: 1.9 (common difference = 0.5)

Be careful to check that your number fits in with the numbers either side of it as well as the sequence in general.

In a variation of the arithmetic progression, two patterns can be combined. For example: 3, 5, 7, 9 and 20, 25, 30, 35 can be combined to give one series: 3, 20, 5, 25, 7, 30, 9, 35, ?
The next number is 11 and the one after that is 40.

Sometimes the difference between consecutive numbers is not constant, but increases (or decreases) for each change. The answer can be predicted by working out how the difference changes.

Example: 1, 3, 6, 10, 15, ?   Answer: 21

- Here the numbers increase by 2, then 3, then 4, then 5 and finally 6 to give 21 as the answer (15 + 6 = 21).

In a variation of the above, the sequence is presented in letters rather than numbers. The question asks for the next letter in the sequence.

Example: find the next letter in the following sequence:
A, C, F, J, ?   Answer: O

ABCDEFGHIJKLMNOPQRSTUVWXYZ
  +2   +3   +4   +5

Finally, if a sequence lacks an obvious pattern then check it for 'prime numbers'. 'Primes' are only divisible by themselves and 1.

Example: find the missing number in the following series:

17, 19, 23, ?, 31, 37   - Here is looks as if the numbers increase by +2, +3, +4 making 27 the missing number 27. However, +5 would give 27 + 5 = 32 (not 31) and +6 would give 38 (not 39).

The answer is actually 29 (the next prime number):
2, 3, 5, 7, 11, 13, 17, 19, 23, 29, 31, 37, 41, 43, 47, 53, 59, 61.

In the following example the numbers look random; however, when adjacent pairs are added together there is a pattern:

11   12   13   10   9   14   17   ?   Answer: 6
    (23)   (23)   (23)   (23)

The Geometrical Progression (G.P.)

In a geometrical progression consecutive numbers are linked by a *common ratio.* To get from one number to the next one you multiply by the common ratio.

i) 1 2 4 8 16 32 ?   Answer 64
Common ratio = 2 = multiply by 2

ii) 80 40 20 10 5 ?   Answer 2.5
Common ratio = 0.5 = divide by 2

iii) 2000 200 20 2 ?   Answer 0.2
Common ratio = 0.1 = divide by 10

As with arithmetic progressions, two geometric progressions can be combined, for example:
2 80 4 40 8 20 16 10 32 ?   Answer 5

In another type of series the numbers increase by a constantly increasing ratio, for example.
5 10 30 120 ?   Answer 600
(ratio = x2, x3, x4, x5 etc)
In the following example the numbers increase by a common ratio plus a constant number (double and add one).

1   3   7   15   31   ?   Answer 63
(1x2+1) (3x2+1) (7x2+1) (15x2+1) (31x2+1)

In the next example the numbers follow a sequence of squares:

1   4   9   ?   25   36   Answer 16
(1^2 2^2 3^2 4^2 5^2 6^2)

Here they follow a sequence of cubes:

1   8   27   64   ?   216   Answer 125
(1^3 2^3 3^3 4^3 5^3 6^3)

2. Patterns with diagrams

In diagrammatic or abstract reasoning questions you need to identify the next shape/missing shape in a sequence of shapes, or work out the analogous relationship between pairs of shapes. The patterns that link shapes together can be numerous and varied and typically include one, or occasionally more than one of the following rules:

Shapes with a reflection (or line) symmetry.
Shapes with rotational symmetry.
Shapes even in number or odd in number in the cell.
Shapes that are similar in shape but different in size.
Shapes with a shaded/unshaded pair.
Shapes with straight lines only/curved lines only.
Shapes with equal/different numbers of sides.
Shapes with equal/different number of shaded regions.
Shapes with equal/different number of intersections (crossover points) or overlapping regions.
Shapes with a right-angle (90 degrees)/no right angles.
Shapes positioned in a row or column in the cell.

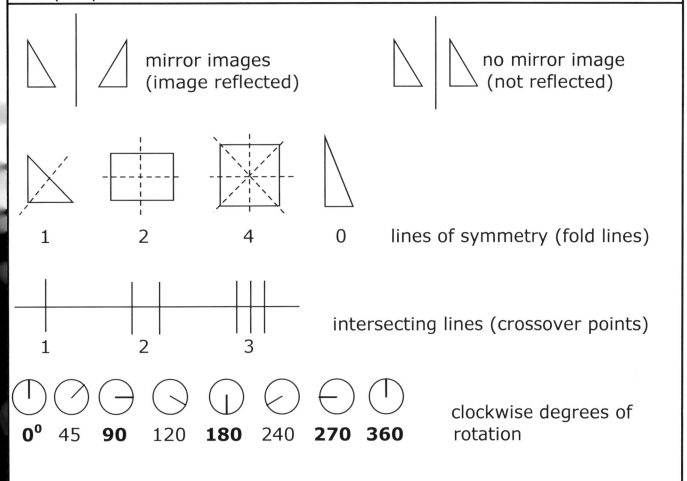

PRACTICE TEST 1

Part 1: Reasoning

Part 2: Verbal Ability

Part 3: Numerical

Part 4: Mechanical

PART 1: REASONING TEST 1 (30 questions in 9 minutes).

RQ1 FRACTION is the opposite of...

A	B	C	D	E
PART	MOST	WHOLE	SOME	MANY

RQ2 PERMANENT means the same as...

A	B	C	D	E
TEMPORARY	BRIEF	EPHEMERAL	LASTING	RELIABLE

RQ3 CHURCH is to WORSHIP as CASINO is to...

A	B	C	D	E
MONEY	SPEND	PRAYER	FAITH	GAMBLE

RQ4

⬡ is to △ as ⯃ is to...

A	B	C	D	E

RQ5

From ⬡ take ◇

and there is left...

A	B	C	D	E

RQ6   Consider this sequence of shapes:

Which of the following comes next?

A	B	C	D	E

_____R

Q7   Consider this sequence of numbers: 23, 34, 45, 56...
Which of the following comes next?

A	B	C	D	E
57	66	68	67	89

_____R

Q8   Consider this sequence of numbers: 28, 31, 29, 32, 30, 33...
Which of the following comes next?

A	B	C	D	E
31	34	29	32	35

RQ9

9 is to 27 as 14 is to...

A	B	C	D	E
40	45	38	42	48

RQ10

50 is to 20 as 200 is to...

A	B	C	D	E
80	100	60	70	120

RQ11   DEVOUT means the same as...

A	B	C	D	E
FOCUSSED	RELIGIOUS	WORTHY	GRACEFUL	DETERMINED

RQ12   LIKE is the opposite of ...

A	B	C	D	E
SIMILAR	POPULAR	LOATHE	PLEASANT	FAVOURITE

RQ13   STREET is to ROAD as ? is to RIVER

A	B	C	D	E
SEA	CANAL	LAKE	SPRING	STREAM

RQ14

Which of the following shapes is the odd one out?

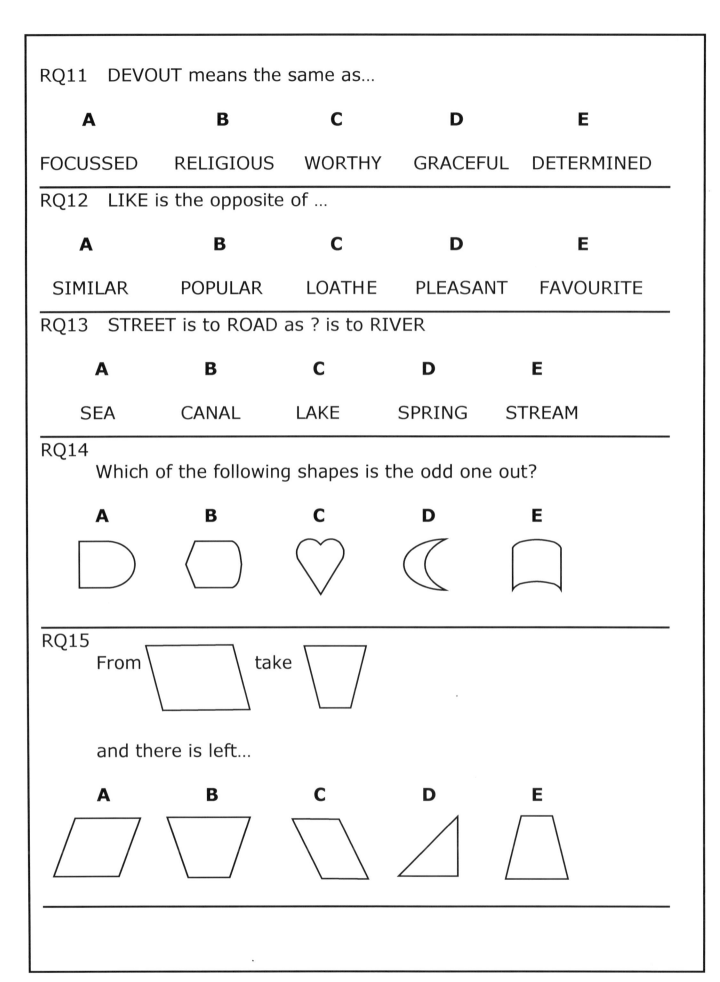

RQ15

From ⬭ take ⬭

and there is left...

RQ16   Consider this sequence of shapes:

Which of the following comes next?

A	B	C	D	E

_____R

Q17   Consider this sequence of numbers: 12, 34, 56, 78,
Which of the following comes next?

A	B	C	D	E
100	110	98	106	102

_____R

Q18   Consider this sequence of numbers: 3, 7, 12, 18...
Which of the following comes next?

A	B	C	D	E
27	25	30	21	22

RQ19

20 is to 4 as 100 is to...

A	B	C	D	E
10	16	20	25	40

RQ20

1 is to 4.5 as 3 is to...

A	B	C	D	E
2/3	1.5	15	14	13.5

RQ21   DISGUISE means the same as...

A	B	C	D	E
REVEAL	CONCEAL	SHOW	EXPLAIN	REQUEST

RQ22   DISSMISIVE is the opposite of...

A	B	C	D	E
INTERESTED	BLASE	APATHETIC	PASSIVE	SCORNFUL

RQ23   GAS is to SOLID as STEAM is to...

A	B	C	D	E
VAPOUR	SNOW	WATER	ICE	LIQUID

RQ24

RQ25

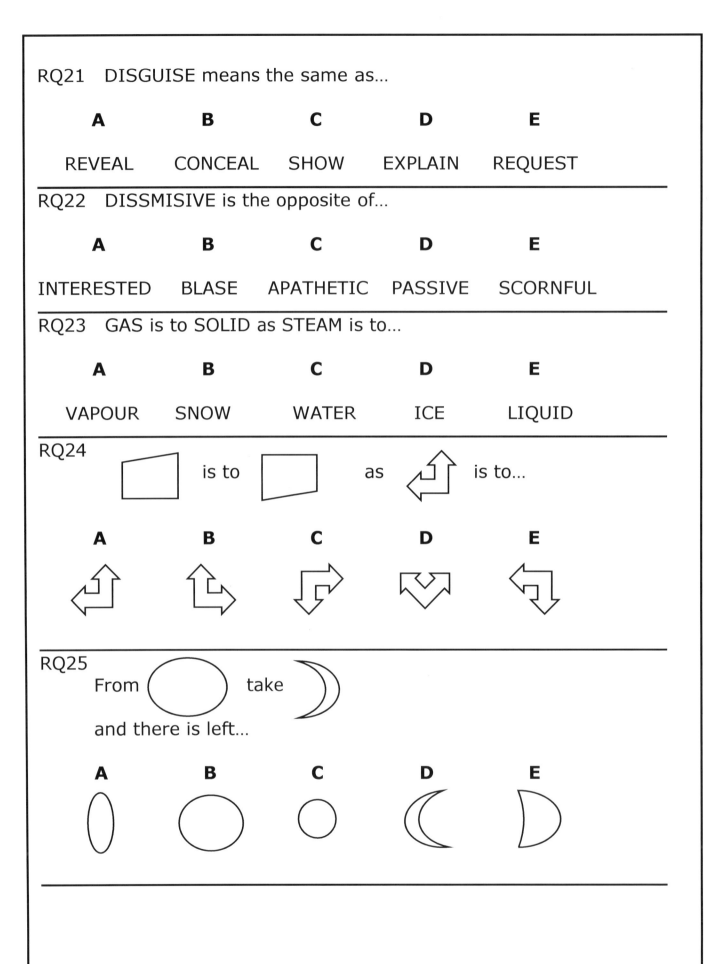

RQ26   Consider this sequence of shapes:

Which of the following comes next?

A	B	C	D	E

_____R

Q27   Consider this sequence of numbers: 95, 83, 72, 60, 49...
Which of the following comes next?

A	B	C	D	E
38	39	36	37	40

_____R

Q28   Consider this sequence of numbers: 1, 17, 33, 49...
Which of the following comes next?

A	B	C	D	E
63	67	64	66	65

RQ29

12.5 is to 2.5 as 150 is to...

A	B	C	D	E
25	30	40	45	32

RQ30

18 is to 12 as ? is to 8

A	B	C	D	E
6	10	8	24	12

PART 2: VERBAL ABILITY TEST 1 (30 questions in 9 minutes).

In the questions below, the word outside the bracket will go with only four of the words inside the bracket to make a longer word. Which **one** word will it **not** go with?

VQ1	A	B	C	D	E
off	(end	shoot	later	shore	beat)

VQ2	A	B	C	D	E
port	(able	hole	side	wine	folio)

VQ3	A	B	C	D	E
in	(ability	operable	frequently	visible	necessary)

In the questions below, which **one** word has a meaning that extends to or includes the meaning of all the others?

VQ4	A	B	C	D	E
	sport	football	golf	rugby	tennis

VQ5	A	B	C	D	E
	petrol	fuel	coal	diesel	paraffin

VQ6	A	B	C	D	E
	rose	tulip	daisy	daffodil	flower

In the questions below, four of the five sentences have the same meaning. Which **one** sentence has a **different** meaning?

VQ7

A   Candidates will fail if they are unfit.
B   Lack of fitness is a reason for failure.
C   Some candidates are unfit to apply.
D   Not every applicant is fit enough to succeed.
E   Applicants will fail if they are unfit.

VQ8

A   He was looking looked forward to his induction day in July.
B   His induction day in July was something to look forward to.
C   He looked forward to his induction in July.
D   July's induction day was something he looked forward to.
E   In July he would look forward to his induction day.

In the questions below, the sentence has a word missing. Which **one** word makes the best sense of the sentence?

VQ9
Becoming an officer is the................of many ambitious recruits.

A	B	C	D	E
decision	possibility	choice	aspiration	desire

VQ10
It is important to make................use of business resources.

A	B	C	D	E
optimum	frequent	tailored	thorough	little

From the five alternatives choose **one** which does not belong with the others.

VQ11

A	B	C	D	E
yielding	rigid	flexible	bending	compliant

VQ12

A	B	C	D	E
clever	bright	adept	naive	smart

VQ13

A	B	C	D	E
bar	block	brick	hamper	prevent

In the questions below, the word outside the bracket is similar to **one** of the words inside the bracket. Which **one** word is it similar to?

VQ14

	A	B	C	D	E
veto	(agree	permit	licence	assist	reject)

VQ15

	A	B	C	D	E
unsure	(certain	doubtful	convinced	positive	confident)

VQ16

	A	B	C	D	E
exempt	(liable	responsible	excused	obliged	necessary)

In the questions below, one of the answers goes with both words to make two new words. Which **one** word fits both words?

VQ17				
	A	**B**	**C**	**D**
green..............plant	(field	keeper	house	grocer)

VQ18				
	A	**B**	**C**	**D**
wood..............fill	(land	work	back	over)

VQ19				
	A	**B**	**C**	**D**
board..............about	(with	run	walk	room)

VQ20				
	A	**B**	**C**	**D**
ship..............ship	(wreck	owner	sails	captain)

In the questions below, one of the answers fits with the pair of words inside the bracket. Which **one** word fits the pair?

VQ21				
	A	**B**	**C**	**D**
(new and fresh)	money	shoes	books	ideas

VQ22				
	A	**B**	**C**	**D**
(wheat and rice)	puddings	cereals	cakes	meals

VQ23				
	A	**B**	**C**	**D**
(paint and scheme)	colour	tin	plan	shade

In the sentences below, which word or words are missing?

VQ24
Many people………………… that the numerical test was the most difficult.

A	B	C	D	E
believe	know	explain	discuss	state

VQ25
They started sooner than us and completed…………………task first.

A	B	C	D	E
there	their	you're	those	they're

VQ26
He is going to finish before we…………this time.

A	B	C	D	E
does	were	was	do	is

VQ27
I'm not sure and I don't think……………really sure either.

A	B	C	D	E
you	your	your'e	yous	you're

VQ28
If it…………………for the traffic, they would have arrived earlier.

A	B	C	D	E
weren't	was	hadn't been	had not	were

The sentences below have a word missing. Which **one** word makes the best sense of the sentence.

VQ29
The best performing schools area often found in........................areas which leads to a lack of fairness in the state school system.

A	B	C	D	E
prosperous	deprived	outdoor	rural	suburban

VQ30
Building stone walls is....................work that requires a high level of fitness and the wearing of protective footwear.

A	B	C	D	E
repetitive	tedious	rewarding	heavy	light

PART 3: NUMERACY TEST 1 (30 questions in 16 minutes).

NQ1   Add 426 to 3765

A	B	C	D	E
5291	3281	4181	4291	4191

NQ2   What is 0.75 expressed as a fraction?

A	B	C	D	E
2/5	3/4	1/2	5/8	2/3

NQ3   The circumference of the earth is 21,639 nautical miles.
What is the circumference correct to three significant numbers?

A	B	C	D	E
21600	216	21630	22000	21640

NQ4   A football pitch is twice as long as it is wide. If the pitch is 50
metres wide the perimeter of the pitch in metres is:

A	B	C	D	E
500	5000	300	150	400

NQ5   What is 22 x 45?

A	B	C	D	E
900	990	910	9090	1020

NQ6   A candidate scored 80% in a test. If the maximum possible mark was 120, then the candidate's mark was:

A	B	C	D	E
84	100	72	102	96

NQ7   If $x = 20$, $y = 14$ and $z = 24$, then $z - x + y =$

A	B	C	D	E
30	10	16	18	24

NQ8 $1/2 \times 1/3 =$

A	B	C	D	E
1/6	2/6	1/5	5/6	1/12

NQ9   If the large (minute) hand of a clock turns by 15 minutes, through how many degrees has it turned?

A	B	C	D	E
60	180	45	360	90

NQ10   One nautical mile = 1.15077945 miles.
What distance is this correct to three decimal places?

A	B	C	D	E
1.151	1.15	1.1508	1.20	1.1

NQ11 600 x 0.25 =

A	B	C	D	E
250	120	150	180	325

NQ12 3522 - 489 =

A	B	C	D	E
3123	3022	3033	3043	3013

NQ13 What is 2/5 expressed as a decimal?

A	B	C	D	E
0.5	0.3	0.25	0.4	0.2

NQ14 What is 3.14159 corrected to three significant figures?

A	B	C	D	E
3.142	3.14	3.1	3.146	3.143

NQ15 If the area of a square play area is 144 m^2. What is the perimeter of the play area in metres?

A	B	C	D	E
72	144	48	96	60

NQ16 What is 575 ÷ 25?

A	B	C	D	E
23	20	22	25	24

NQ17 A pupil has £111 in savings. If she spends 10% of it, how much is left?

A	B	C	D	E
£100	£99	£98.90	£99.90	£99.99

NQ18 If $x = 29$ and y is three times x then $y - x =$

A	B	C	D	E
76	58	68	78	81

NQ19 $2\frac{1}{2} + 4\frac{3}{4} =$

A	B	C	D	E
$7\frac{1}{4}$	$6\frac{1}{2}$	$6\frac{3}{4}$	$6\frac{1}{4}$	$6\frac{1}{8}$

NQ20 If the large (hour) hand of a clock turns by 40 minutes, through how many degrees has it turned?

A	B	C	D	E
135	200	220	240	175

NQ21 Round 0.00567 correct to two significant figures

A	B	C	D	E
0.05	0.01	0.057	0.0056	0.0057

NQ22 4000 x 0.001 =

A	B	C	D	E
40	4	0.4	0.04	400

NQ23 When mixing mortar the sand to cement ratio is 4:1 by volume. How many cubic metres of cement are needed need to make one cubic metre of mortar?

A	B	C	D	E
0.8	1.0	4	0.2	0.25

NQ24 One-third to three decimal places is 0.333, whereas two-thirds to three decimal places is:

A	B	C	D	E
0.666	0.6667	0.667	0.67	0.66

NQ25 What is 3/8 as a percentage?

A	B	C	D	E
39%	42.5%	38%	38.5%	37.5%

NQ26 $\dfrac{1}{2} \div \dfrac{3}{8} =$

A	B	C	D	E
$1\dfrac{1}{3}$	$1\dfrac{1}{2}$	$1\dfrac{1}{4}$	$1\dfrac{2}{3}$	$1\dfrac{1}{6}$

NQ27 What is the highest common factor of 12 and 18?

A	B	C	D	E
6	12	8	2	4

NQ28 If 1 km = 5/8 of a mile, how far is 96 km in miles?

A	B	C	D	E
24	48	60	72	68

NQ29 If the minute (large) hand of a clock makes 2.5 complete revolutions, by how many degrees does it turn through?

A	B	C	D	E
180	900	540	360	120

NQ30 If the hour (small) hand of a clock turns through 4 hours, by how many degrees does it turn through?

A	B	C	D	E
160	135	150	120	90

PART 4: MECHANICAL TEST 1 (30 questions in 10 minutes).

MQ1 How will these two magnets behave when they are brought together?

A Attract
B Repel
C Neither attract nor repel
D Can't say

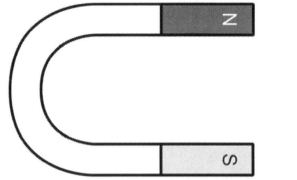

MQ2 Which shape has its centre of mass nearest the ground?

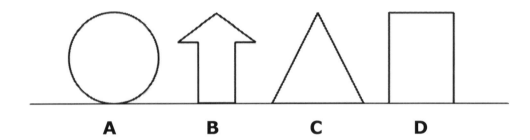

     A   **B**   **C**   **D**

MQ3 How much force (F) is required to lift the 420 kg trailer?

A 70 kg
B 60 kg
C 140 kg
D 420 kg

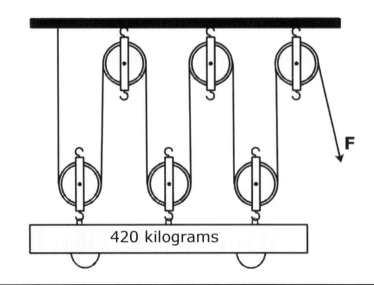

420 kilograms

MQ4 All three circuits contain identical bulbs and batteries. When the switches are closed, which circuit's bulbs glow the brightest? (if all the same, mark D).

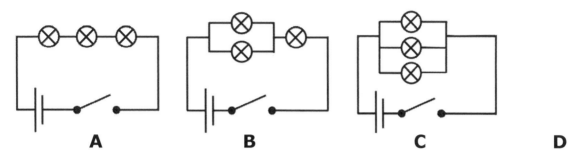

A   B   C   D

MQ5 At which point will the beam balance?

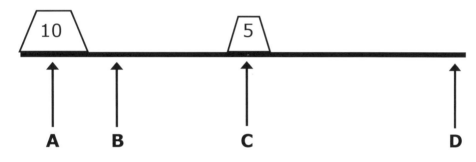

A   B   C   D

MQ6 In which vessel is the water pressure the lowest at the bottom? (if all same, mark D).

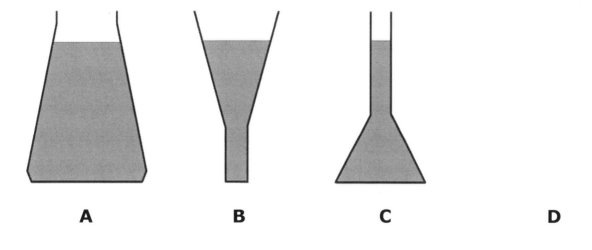

A   B   C   D

MQ7 If all the valves are open, which valve(s) **must** be closed so that
     all the gas flows from the high pressure cylinder (P) to fill the
     low pressure cylinder (p) via the pressure gauge (Pg)?

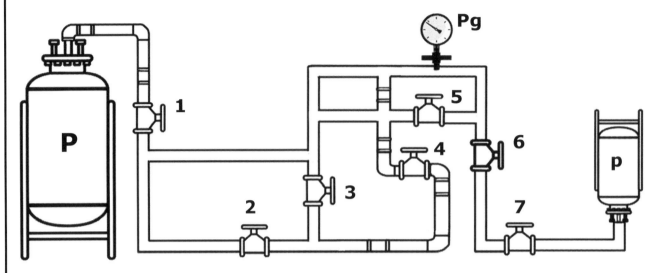

A 2, 3, 4 and 5
B 2, 3 and 5
C 5 only
D 3 and 4

MQ8 If steam under pressure enters the cylinder at A, then B, then A
     again, how will the piston move?

A left, right, left
B left, right, stop
C right, left, right
D right, stop, left

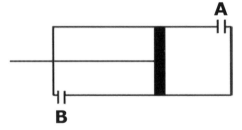

MQ9 What type of pressure is exerted on a submerged submarine?

A atmospheric
B hydraulic
C pneumatic
D hydrostatic

MQ10   These three containers each hold two litres of water when full.
If they are filled at the same rate, which container will reach
the level of the dashed line first? (if all the same, mark D).

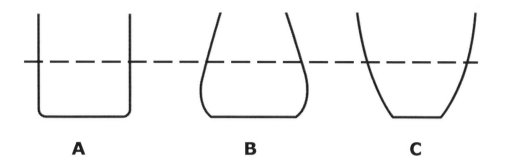

A   B   C   D

MQ11   In the following circuit you could increase the current by:

A 'shorting out' a bulb
B adding a bulb
C removing a bulb
D using a less powerful bulb

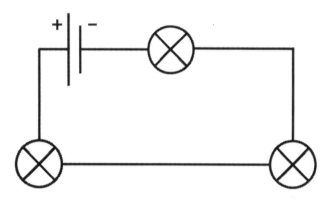

MQ12   In which tank is the pressure the highest at the bottom? (if all
the same, mark D).

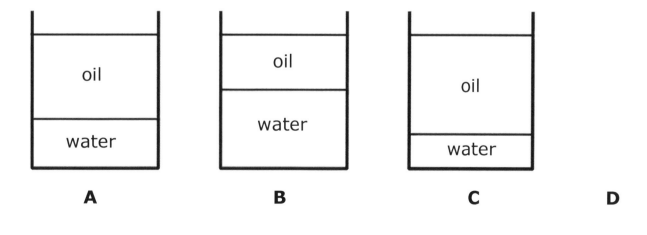

A   B   C   D

MQ13 When the connecting rod moves to the right, which gears turn anti-clockwise?

A 3 only
B 1 and 2
C 2 only
D 1 and 3

MQ14 If the first ball drops out of the cannon and hits the ground two seconds later, at what speed must the second ball have left the cannon if it travelled 200 metres before hitting the ground?

A 50 metres/sec
B 100 metres/sec
C 200 metres/sec
D 300 metres/sec

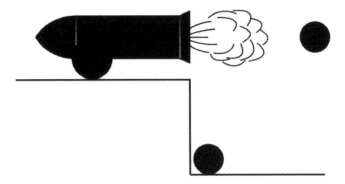

MQ15 If gear number 1 turns at 240 rpm, how fast is gear 9 turning?

A 80 rpm
B 120 rpm
C 160 rpm
D 240 rpm

MQ16 In this pulley system how much load does each rope support?

A 2 kg
B 2.5 kg
C 4 kg
D 10 kg

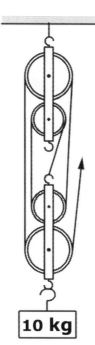

MQ17 If switch 1 is closed and switch 2 remains open, which bulbs will illuminate?

A Bulbs B and D
B Bulbs B, C and D
C Bulbs A, B and C
D Bulbs A, B and D

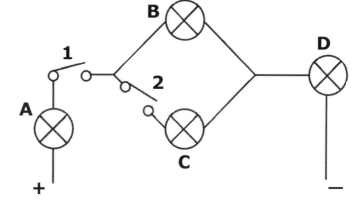

MQ18 The symbol shown below represents an electrical component that stores energy between two parallel plates. What is it?

A a battery
B a capacitor
C an inductor
D a thermistor

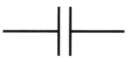

MQ19 When the switch is closed, how many bulbs will illuminate if bulb 1 is removed?

A 0
B 1
C 2
D 3

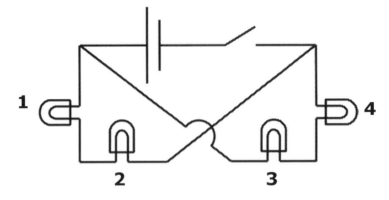

MQ20 When the tap is opened it takes exactly 30 seconds to drain the tank of half of its contents. How long does it take to empty the tank completely?

A 1 minute
B less than 1 minute
C more than 1 minute
D impossible to say

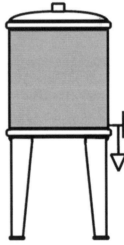

MQ21 If bulb 4 is removed, what will happen?

A no bulbs illuminate
B one bulb illuminates
C two bulbs illuminate
D three bulbs illuminate

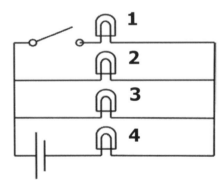

MQ22 How many switches should be closed to illuminate two bulbs?

A 1
B 2
C 3
D 4

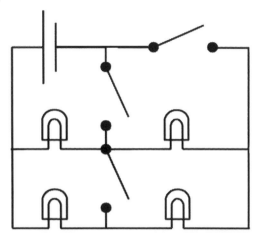

MQ23 The symbol shown below represents an electrical component that restricts the flow of current to one direction. What is it?

A a diode
B an inductor
C a transistor
D a resistor

MQ24 At which height off the ground does the falling ball have the most energy? (if all the same, mark D).

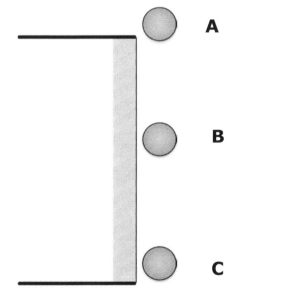

A

B

C   D

MQ25 Three identical springs, connected in series, stretch by a total of 12 cm when a force of 50 Newton's is applied. How far does one of the springs stretch under the same force?

A 4 cm
B 12 cm
C 24 cm
D 36 cm

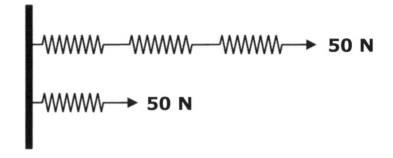

MQ26 If wheel '1' is spinning clockwise, how are wheels 2 and 3 spinning viewed from the end of their shaft's.

A both clockwise
B both anti-clockwise
C 2 anti-clockwise, 3 clockwise
D 2 clockwise, 3 anti-clockwise

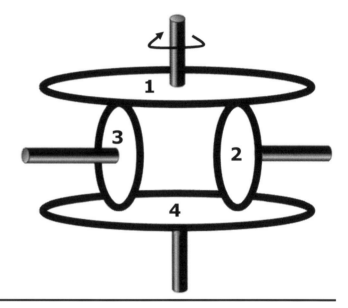

MQ27 If this steam engine is travelling right to left, how are gears 2 and 4 rotating?

A both anti-clockwise
B both clockwise
C 2 clockwise, 4 anti-clockwise
D 2 anti-clockwise, 4 clockwise

MQ28 Which countries' hot air balloon will rise at the fastest rate or can carry the greatest load? (if all the same mark D).

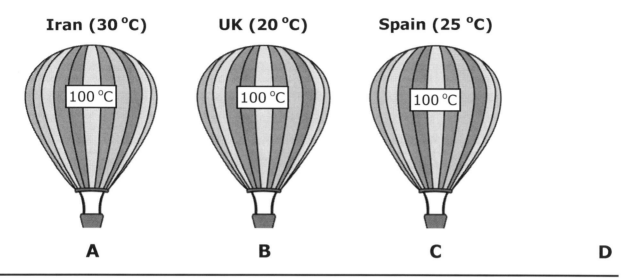

Iran (30 °C)   **UK (20 °C)**   **Spain (25 °C)**

100 °C   100 °C   100 °C

A   **B**   **C**   **D**

MQ29 How heavy is weight 'X' if the lever is balanced?

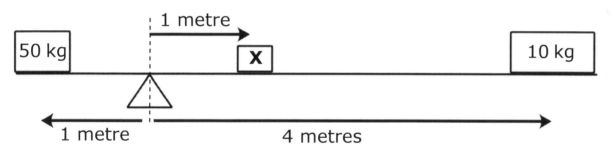

1 metre

50 kg   X   10 kg

1 metre   4 metres

A 2 kg
B 4 kg
C 5 kg
D 10 kg

MQ30 The large gears have twice as many teeth as the small gears. If gear 'X' turns at 20 rpm, how quickly does gear 'Y' turn?

A 2 rpm
B 3 rpm
C 4 rpm
D 5 rpm

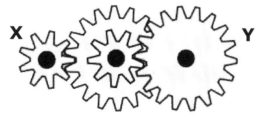

X   Y

PRACTICE TEST 2

Part 1: Reasoning

Part 2: Verbal Ability

Part 3: Numerical

Part 4: Mechanical

PART 1: REASONING TEST 2 (30 questions in 9 minutes).

RQ1   AUTHENTIC means the same as...

A	**B**	**C**	**D**	**E**
REAL	IDENTICAL	FALSE	FLIMSY	NEW

RQ2   UNIFORM is the opposite of ...

A	**B**	**C**	**D**	**E**
STEADY	DIFFERENT	EVEN	SHABBY	CONSTANT

RQ3 CIRCLE is to SQUARE as SPHERE is to...

A	**B**	**C**	**D**	**E**
CYLINDER	GLOBE	PYRAMID	CUBE	PRISM

RQ4

RQ5

Which of the following shapes is the odd one out?

RQ6   Consider this sequence of shapes:

Which of the following comes next?

A	B	C	D	E

_____R

Q7   Consider this sequence of numbers: 203, 35, 193, 45...
Which of the following comes next?

A	B	C	D	E
55	172	183	182	184

_____R

Q8   Consider this sequence of numbers: 9, 16, 25, 36, 49...
Which of the following comes next?

A	B	C	D	E
72	64	81	100	66

RQ9

1/2 is to 1/4 as 1/3 is to...

A	B	C	D	E
2/3	1/8	5/6	1/6	1/2

RQ10

0.25 is to 2.5 as 0.125 is to...

A	B	C	D	E
10	12.5	1.25	2.5	5

RQ11   ROBUST means the same as...

A	B	C	D	E
REGULAR	REFINED	RELIABLE	RECEPTIVE	RESILIENT

RQ12   RESTRICT is the opposite of...

A	B	C	D	E
FREE	SHELTER	CURB	ENCLOSE	DENY

RQ13   BOOK is to LIBRARY as PAINTING is to...

A	B	C	D	E
MUSEUM	ART	PORTRAIT	EASEL	GALLERY

RQ14

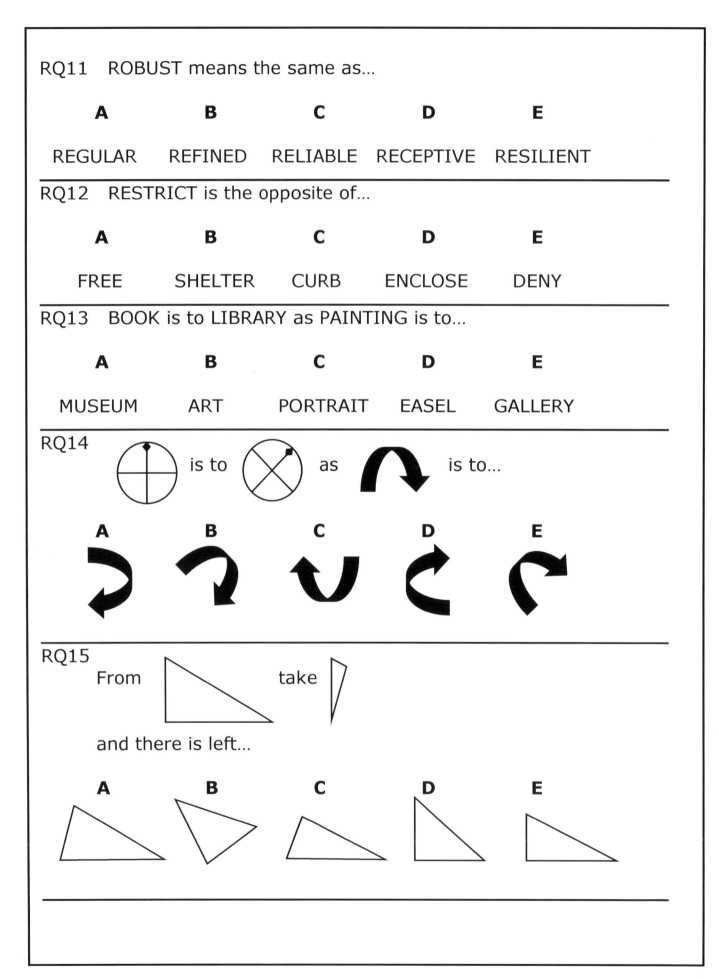

RQ15

From ⬜ take ⬜ and there is left...

RQ16   Consider this sequence of shapes:

Which of the following comes next?

A	B	C	D	E

RQ17 Consider this sequence of numbers: 12, 20, 24, 19, 36, 18...
Which of the following comes next?

A	B	C	D	E
17	28	26	48	40

RQ18 Consider this sequence of numbers: 5, 10, 20, 35, 55...
Which two numbers come next?

A	B	C	D	E
80,95	75,110	90,125	85,130	80,110

RQ19
    40 is to 60 as 30 is to...

A	B	C	D	E
50	45	48	36	55

RQ20
    1/5 is to 12 as 1/6 is to...

A	B	C	D	E
10	8	9	15	20

RQ21   ACCOMPLISH means the same as...

A	B	C	D	E
ABANDON	FORFEIT	BEGIN	QUESTION	ACHIEVE

RQ22 DETRIMENT is the opposite of ...

A	B	C	D	E
DAMAGE	HANDICAP	LOSS	ADVANTAGE	PREJUDICE

RQ23 TYRE is to RUBBER as WHEEL is to...

A	B	C	D	E
CAR	ALLOY	RIM	HUB	SPOKE

RQ24

A	B	C	D	E

RQ25

From take

and there is left...

A	B	C	D	E

RQ26 Which of the following shapes is the odd one out?

| A | B | C | D | E |

RQ27 Consider this sequence of numbers: 16, 19, 23, 28, 34...
Which of the following pairs of numbers comes next?

A	B	C	D	E
40,48	42,49	32,40	30,38	41,49

RQ28 Consider this sequence of numbers: 2.7, 3.2, 4.2, 5.7, 7.7...
Which of the following comes next?

A	B	C	D	E
10.7	11.7	10.2	9.7	11.2

RQ29
   4 is to 3 as 120 is to...

A	B	C	D	E
75	90	72	80	64

RQ30
   0.1 is to 6 as 0.25 is to...

A	B	C	D	E
125	1.25	1.5	15	12

PART 2: VERBAL ABILITY TEST 2 (30 questions in 9 minutes).

In the questions below, the word outside the bracket will go with only four of the words inside the bracket to make a longer word. Which **one** word will it **not** go with?

VQ1

	A	B	C	D	E
home	(sick	land	less	work	bargain)

VQ2

	A	B	C	D	E
no	(way	table	thing	body	blest)

VQ3

	A	B	C	D	E
over	(night	grown	difficult	time	take)

In the questions below, which **one** word has a meaning that extends to or includes the meaning of all the others?

VQ4

A	B	C	D	E
cottage	dwelling	flat	bungalow	mansion

VQ5

A	B	C	D	E
healthy	safe	disinfected	clean	hygienic

VQ6

A	B	C	D	E
oxygen	acetylene	butane	gas	propane

In the questions below, four of the five sentences have the same meaning. Which **one** sentence has a **different** meaning?

VQ7

A Menu: pie and chips; baked potato with beans.
B Menu: baked potato and beans, or pie and chips.
C Menu: pie with chips, beans and baked potato.
D Menu: pie and chips, or baked potato with beans.
E Menu: pie with chips, or beans and baked potato.

VQ8

A The red car ran into the back of the blue car.
B The blue car was struck by the back of the red car.
C It was the blue car that was hit from behind by the red one.
C The red car collided with the blue car from behind.
E The blue car had a rear–end shunt from a red car.

VQ9

A We must leave early enough to arrive before midnight.
B To arrive before midnight we need to make an early start.
C We will depart early to arrive before 24:00 hours.
D Arrival before midnight is necessary for an early start.
E Arriving before 24:00 hours is possible with an early start.

VQ10

A Mike will probably attend class tomorrow.
B It is unlikely that Mike will not attend tomorrow's class.
C Mike's class is not expected until tomorrow.
D Tomorrow, Mike is expected to be in class.
E Mike will almost certainly attend the class tomorrow.

In the questions below, the sentence has a word missing. Which **one** word makes the best sense of the sentence?

VQ11
Too much saturated fat is our diets is................with an increased risk of heart disease.

A	B	C	D	E
found	associated	attributed	responsible	known

VQ12
Following the arrest,................with Scotland Yard would be necessary.

A	B	C	D	E
discussion	contact	work	appeals	liaison

From the five alternatives choose **one** word which does not belong with the others.

VQ13

A	B	C	D	E
powerful	strong	frail	robust	tough

VQ14

A	B	C	D	E
sand	sea	air	road	rail

VQ15

A	B	C	D	E
student	teacher	pupil	scholar	learner

In the questions below, the word outside the bracket is similar to **one** of the words inside the bracket. Which **one** word is it similar to?

VQ16

	A	B	C	D	E
punctual	(early	late	slow	delayed	tardy)

VQ17

	A	B	C	D	E
relevant	(needed	suited	necessary	useful	helpful)

VQ18

	A	B	C	D	E
clear	(cloudy	opaque	hazy	transparent	vague)

In the questions below, one of the answers goes with both words to make two new words. Which **one** word fits both words?

VQ19

	A	B	C	D
house..............load	(boat	heavy	motor	brick)

VQ20

	A	B	C	D
run..............ward	(along	for	way	wind)

VQ21

	A	B	C	D
key..............lock	(board	canal	safe	pad)

VQ22

	A	B	C	D
out..............dated	(source	back	crop	up)

In the questions below, one of the answers fits with the pair of words inside the bracket. Which **one** word fits the pair?

VQ23	A	B	C	D
(ferry and deliver)	ship	boat	sail	parcel

VQ24	A	B	C	D
(shape and transform)	box	triangle	move	change

VQ25	A	B	C	D
(upset and alarm)	worry	ill	bell	knock

In the questions below, which word or words are missing?

VQ26
Some applicants find the tests difficult because………………not prepared.

A	B	C	D	E
there	their	they've	they'd	they'll

VQ27
I think that………………new venues were the ideal place to meet.

A	B	C	D	E
these	those	them	there	this

VQ28
It looks as if the team………………in need of more practice today.

A	B	C	D	E
were	was	we're	are	is

The sentences below have a word missing. Which **one** word makes the best sense of the sentence.

VQ29
The candidates.........................manner made it difficult for the panel to take him seriously.

A	**B**	**C**	**D**	**E**
familiar	sincere	elated	flippant	formal

VQ30
Only by.....................the job advertisement could she identify whether or not the opportunity met her exact requirements.

A	**B**	**C**	**D**	**E**
scrutinizing	browsing	scanning	checking	investigating

PART 3: NUMERACY TEST 2 (30 questions in 16 minutes).

NQ1   3172 – 275 =

A	B	C	D	E
2897	2887	2797	2877	2867

NQ2   What is 45% expressed as a fraction?

A	B	C	D	E
4/5	9/20	4/9	4/11	7/9

NQ3   Lands End to John o' Groats is 1407 km? What is this distance correct to three significant figures?

A	B	C	D	E
1400	1407	1410	140	1500

NQ4   A triangle is 4 cm high with a base 3 cm long. In cm^2, the area of the triangle is:

A	B	C	D	E
12	8	4	6	90

NQ5   What is 32 x 120?

A	B	C	D	E
3800	3620	3480	3760	3840

NQ6 A pupil scored 65% in a test. If the maximum possible mark was 80, then the candidate's mark was:

A	B	C	D	E
56	52	50	42	54

NQ7 If $x = 215$ and $y = 75$ then $y - x =$

A	B	C	D	E
140	135	−135	−150	−140

NQ8 $\dfrac{5}{6} \div \dfrac{5}{8} =$

A	B	C	D	E
$1\dfrac{2}{6}$	11/6	$1\dfrac{1}{6}$	15/6	$1\dfrac{2}{5}$

NQ9 If the large (minute) hand of a clock turns by 50 minutes, through how many degrees has it turned?

A	B	C	D	E
200	240	300	360	270

NQ10 One nautical mile = 1.15077945 miles.
What distance is this correct to three significant figures?

A	B	C	D	E
1.151	1.15	1.157	1.158	1.16

NQ11   250 x 0.04 =

A	B	C	D	E
1	2.5	40	10	0.1

NQ12   A shoe box measures 30 cm x 15 cm x 10 cm. What is its volume in litres?

A	B	C	D	E
0.45	4.5	45	0.045	450

NQ13   What is 19/25 expressed as a decimal?

A	B	C	D	E
0.19	0.38	0.76	0.72	0.75

NQ14   What is 3.14159 corrected to four decimal places?

A	B	C	D	E
3.1416	3.142	3.1425	3.142	3.14

NQ15   The perimeter of a square is 44 cm. What is its area in cm^2?

A	B	C	D	E
110	111	112	121	132

NQ16   What is 1040 ÷ 20?

A	B	C	D	E
54	55	48	46	52

NQ17 How many books costing £8.95 each can be bought for £200?

A	B	C	D	E
20	21	22	23	24

NQ18 If $s = 9$ and $t = 16$ then $s \times t - s =$

A	B	C	D	E
135	151	63	125	136

NQ19 $3\dfrac{3}{4} \times 8 =$

A	B	C	D	E
32	26	25	30	28

NQ20 If the large (minute) hand of a clock turns by 45 minutes, through how many degrees has it turned?

A	B	C	D	E
45	135	95	360	270

NQ21 21.04568 rounded to three significant figures.

A	B	C	D	E
21.007	21	21.05	21.0468	21.046

NQ22   10000 x 0.125 =

A	B	C	D	E
125000	12.5	12500	1250	125

NQ23   50 divided in the ratio 9:1 is:

A	B	C	D	E
45:5	20:10	48:2	50:10	36:14

NQ24   5/9 as a decimal to two decimal places is:

A	B	C	D	E
0.55	0.56	0.555	0.6	0.556

NQ25   What is the area of the shaded region in cm^2?

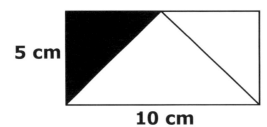

5 cm

10 cm

A	B	C	D	E
50	10	12.5	15	37.5

NQ26 $6 \div \dfrac{3}{7} =$

A	B	C	D	E
21	7	15	18	14

NQ27   What is the lowest common multiple of 6 and 8?

A	B	C	D	E
8	48	18	24	16

NQ28   If 1 mile = 1.6 km of a mile, how far is 25 miles in km?

A	B	C	D	E
20	44	18	32	40

NQ29   If the minute (large) hand of a clock makes 3 complete revolutions, by how many degrees does it turn through?

A	B	C	D	E
1080	540	960	270	1440

NQ30   If the hour (small) hand of a clock turns through 1 hour, by how many degrees does it turn through?

A	B	C	D	E
5^0	50^0	30^0	60^0	12^0

PART 4: MECHANICAL TEST 2 (30 questions in 10 minutes).

MQ1　These three ingots are all the same weight. Which ingot exerts the least pressure on the ground? (if all the same, mark D).

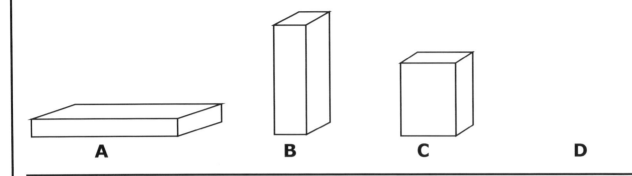

MQ2　Two identical steel balls are moving at the same speed and in opposite directions. What happens after the two balls strike each other in a head-on collision?

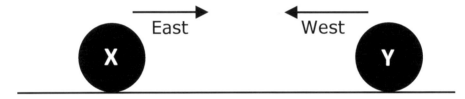

A　　The two balls stop.
B　　'X' moves to the West and 'Y' moves to the East.
C　　'X' moves to the East and 'Y' moves to the West.
D　　Can't tell

MQ3　This three-car coupling is travelling to the left. Which coupling has the highest tension? (if all the same, mark D).

MQ4 In this electrical circuit, which of these identical bulbs will be the brightest?

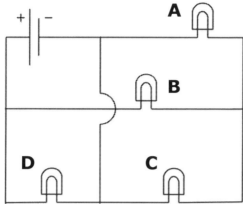

MQ5 Which flight of stairs has the greatest mechanical advantage? (if all the same, mark D).

MQ6 At what position would you need to place the 10 kg weight to balance the lever?

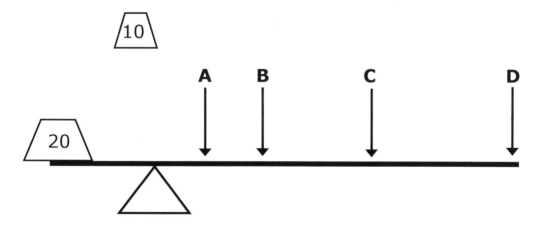

MQ7 If the largest gear spins at a speed of 120 rpm, how fast does the smallest gear spin?

A 180 rpm
B 480 rpm
C 360 rpm
D 240 rpm

MQ8 Which pulley requires the least amount of force (F) to lift the load? (if all the same mark D).

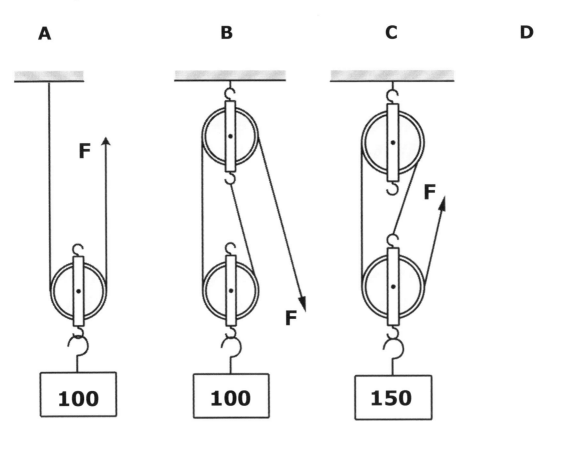

MQ9 If you close both switches, how many bulbs will light?

A 1
B 2
C 3
D 4

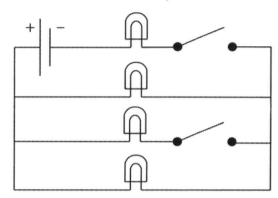

MQ10 If star wheel **5** turns clockwise, which two other wheels turn clockwise?

A 1 and 3
B 2 and 4
C 4 and 6
D 2 and 6

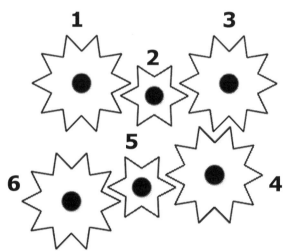

MQ11 What happens to the trolley on the inclined frictionless plane?

A Climbs up
B Rolls down
C Stays still
D Impossible to say

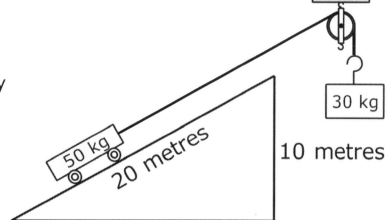

MQ12　In which tank is the water pressure the greatest at the point marked 'X'? (if all the same, mark D).

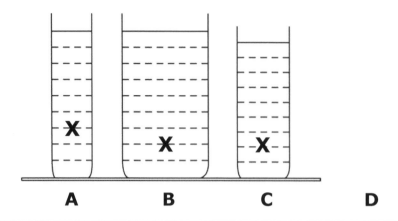

A　　　　**B**　　　　**C**　　　　**D**

MQ13　What weight (**W**) will lift the 5 metric ton lorry if the diameters of the hydraulic pistons are in the ratio 10:1?

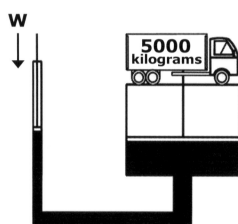

A 50000 kg
B 500 kg
C 50 kg
D 5 kg

MQ14　What is the voltmeter reading if the full-scale deflection (FSD is 240 volts?

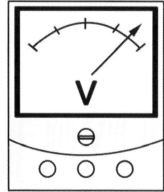

A 160
B 175
C 180
D 210

MQ15 In diagrams of electrical circuits the symbol below is used to represent:

A a light emitting diode
B an earth lead
C a variable resistor
D a positive lead

MQ16 Which of these four solid shapes is the least likely to topple over if it is accidentally knocked?

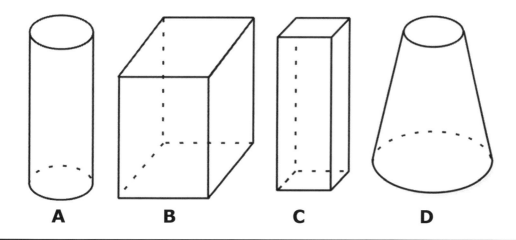

A   **B**   **C**   **D**

MQ17 If gear 'X' rotates clockwise, how does gear 'Y' rotate?

A anti-clockwise, slower than 'X'
B anti-clockwise, same speed as 'X'
C clockwise, same speed as 'X'
D clockwise, slower than 'X'

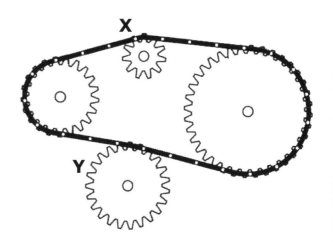

MQ18 How far would you have to pull the rope to drag the load by 1 metre?

A 1 m
B 3 m
C 4 m
D 5 m

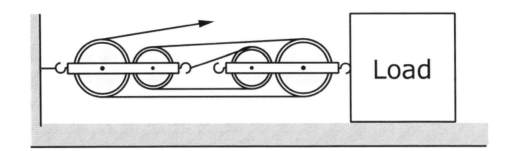

MQ19 What is the voltmeter reading?

A 0 V
B 12 V
C 36 V
D −36 V

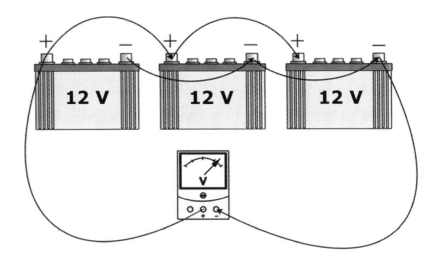

MQ20 What is the voltmeter reading?

A 6 V
B −6 V
C 12 V
D −12 V

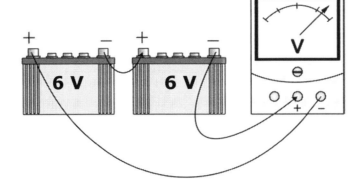

MQ21 On which face of this submerged block is the water pressure the greatest? (if all the same mark D).

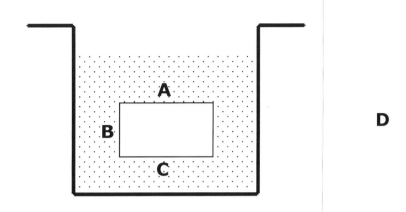

MQ22 Which weight is the heaviest? (if impossible to say, mark D).

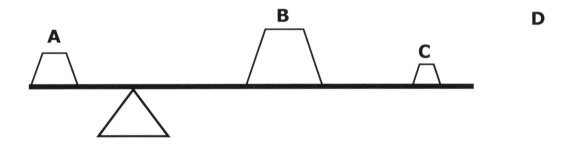

MQ23 Which pencils are in a state of stable equilibrium?

A P2 and P3
B P3 only
C All three
D None

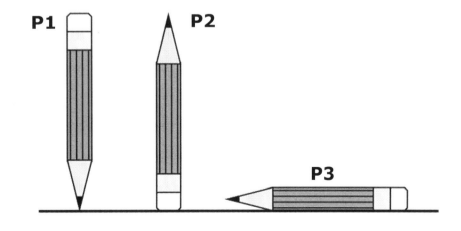

MQ24　If drive wheel 'W' rotates at a constant speed, how does drive
wheel 'Z' rotate?

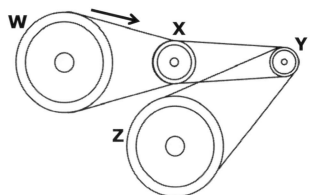

A　clockwise faster than 'W'
B　anti-clockwise same as 'W'
C　clockwise slower than 'W'
D　clockwise same as 'W'

MQ25 Where is the air flowing fastest around this wing section?

MQ26　Which system of springs will stretch the furthest when the
finger is removed (if all the same mark D).

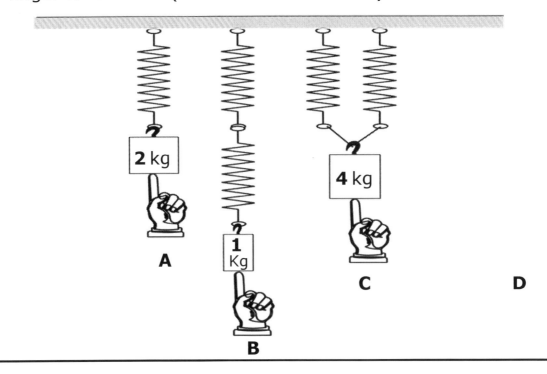

MQ27 A skydiver reaches terminal velocity when the force due to air résistance equals the force due to:

A   **B**   **C**   **D**
Gravity   Friction   Drag   Pressure

MQ28 Mains water flows through a series of pipes and taps as shown. Where is the pressure the lowest? (if all the same mark D).

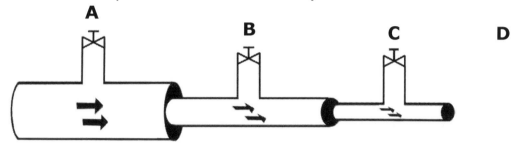

MQ29 A golf ball is driven off a tee. At the top of its flight, the ball:

A has lost all of its kinetic energy
B has no horizontal kinetic energy
C has lost all its energy
D achieves maximum potential energy

MQ30 How heavy is '**X**' in grams if the scales are balanced?

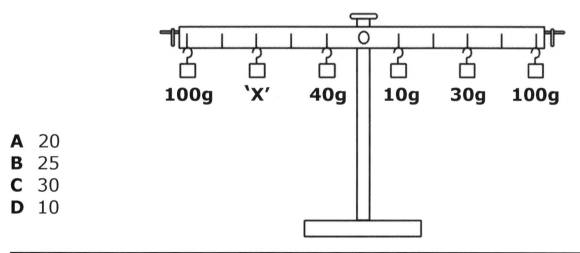

A 20
B 25
C 30
D 10

PRACTICE TEST 3

Part 1: Reasoning

Part 2: Verbal Ability

Part 3: Numerical

Part 4: Mechanical

PART 1: REASONING TEST 3 (30 questions in 9 minutes).

RQ1 ASCERTAIN means the same as...

A	**B**	**C**	**D**	**E**
DETERMINE	QUERY	OVERLOOK	TEST	COMPREHEND

RQ2 COMPRESS is the opposite of ...

A	**B**	**C**	**D**	**E**
SPRING	SQUEEZE	DENSE	STRETCH	CRUSH

RQ3 CAR is to PASSENGERS as SHIP is to...

A	**B**	**C**	**D**	**E**
DRIVER	CARGO	LOAD	CAPTAIN	BOAT

RQ4

is to ◯ as ⬛ is to...

A **B** **C** **D** **E**

RQ5

Which of the following shapes is the odd one out?

A **B** **C** **D** **E**

RQ6   Consider this sequence of shapes:

Which of the following fills the missing space?

A	**B**	**C**	**D**	**E**

R

Q7   Consider this sequence of numbers: 25, 30, 50, 60, 75, 90...
Which of the following pairs of numbers come next?

A	**B**	**C**	**D**	**E**
95,115	105,125	80,100	85,95	100,120

RQ8   Consider this sequence of numbers: 6, 11, 21, 41, 81...
Which of the following comes next?

A	**B**	**C**	**D**	**E**
181	161	141	121	101

RQ9

   75 is to 5 as 60 is to...

A	**B**	**C**	**D**	**E**
5	15	10	4	12

RQ10

   30 is to 100 as 24 is to...

A	**B**	**C**	**D**	**E**
72	75	48	96	80

RQ11   DISMISS means the same as...

A	B	C	D	E
PERMIT	ACCEPT	REJECT	KEEP	RETAIN

RQ12   STRICT is the opposite of ...

A	B	C	D	E
STRINGENT	LENIENT	AUSTERE	HARSH	RIGOROUS

RQ13   ELECTRICITY is to CABLE as WATER is to...

A	B	C	D	E
LAKE	BOTTLE	WIRE	TAP	PIPE

RQ14

Which of the following boxes of shapes is the odd one out?

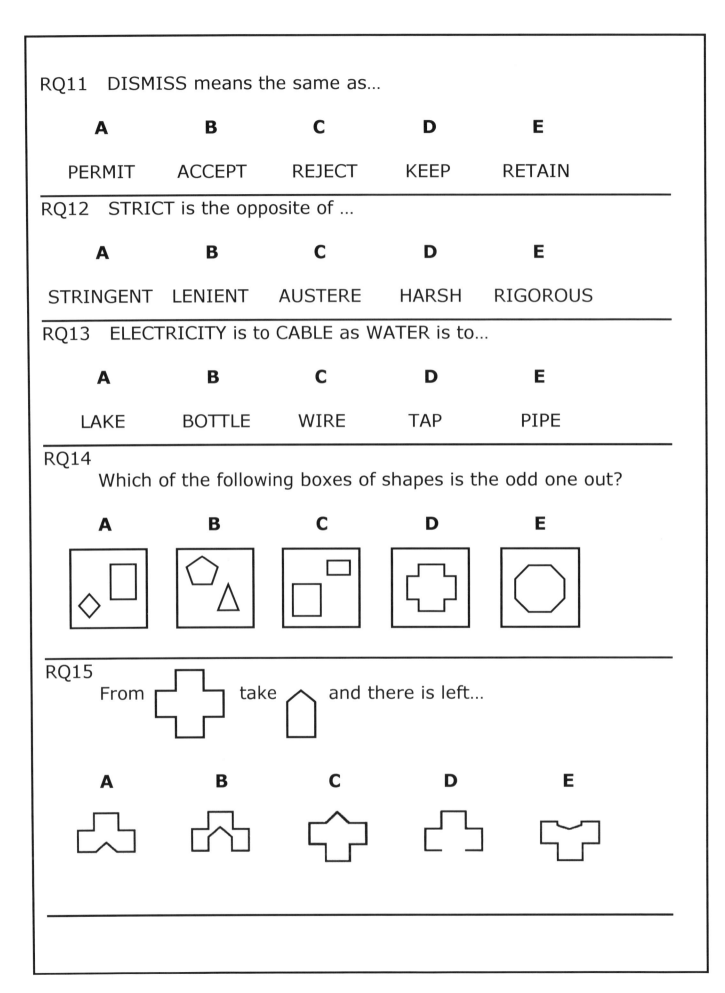

RQ15

From ✛ take ⬠ and there is left...

A   B   C   D   E

RQ16   Consider this sequence of shapes:

Which of the following comes next?

A	B	C	D	E

RQ17   Consider this sequence of numbers: 72, 60, 49, 39...
Which of the following comes next?

A	B	C	D	E
27	29	28	31	30

RQ18   Consider this sequence of numbers: 2, 3, 5, 7, 11, 13...
Which of the following pairs of numbers comes next?

A	B	C	D	E
17,19	12,15	15,17	14,16	16,19

RQ19
   64 is to 8 as 25 is to...

A	B	C	D	E
1	8	4	5	6

RQ20
   0.1 is to 2.25 as 10 is to...

A	B	C	D	E
22.5	0.225	225	2250	2.25

RQ21   INCLINATION means the same as...

A	B	C	D	E
TENDENCY	CERTAINTY	INABILITY	SUITABILITY	INDIFFERENCE

RQ22   OBSTRUCT is the opposite of ...

A	B	C	D	E
STOP	ENCOURAGE	IMPEDE	BARRICADE	SANDBAG

RQ23   CEMENT is to CONCRETE as OXYGEN is to...

A	B	C	D	E
WATER	NITROGEN	AIR	EARTH	BREATH

RQ24

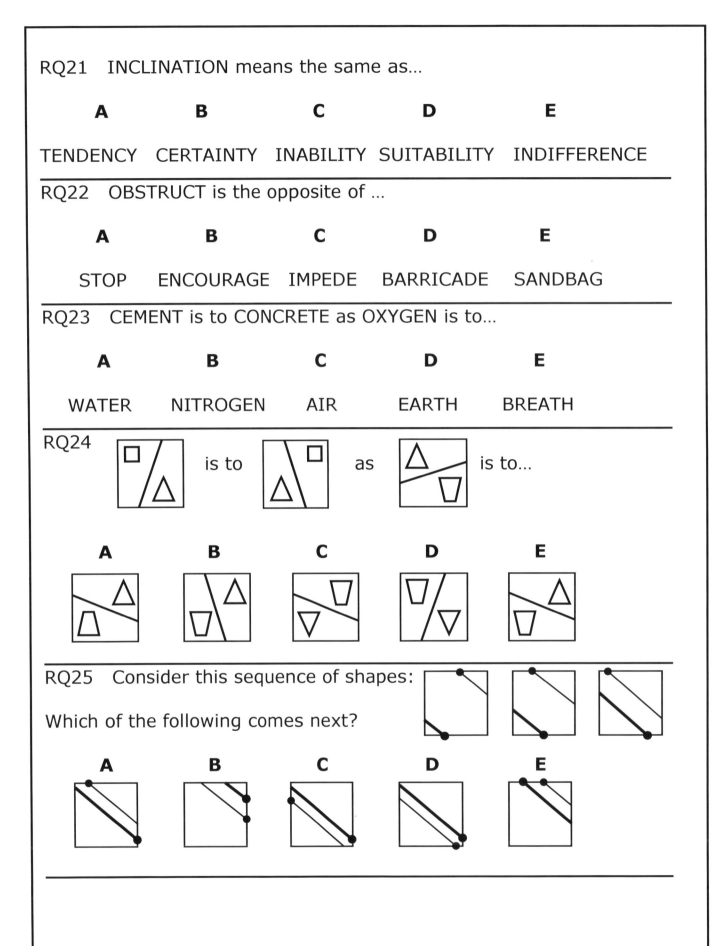

RQ25   Consider this sequence of shapes:

Which of the following comes next?

RQ26 Consider this sequence of shapes:

Which of the following fills the missing space?

A	B	C	D	E

RQ27   Consider this sequence of numbers: 2, 16, 4, 13, 6, 10, 8…
Which of the following comes next?

A	B	C	D	E
10	7	9	8	5

RQ28   Consider this sequence of numbers: 1, 6, 12, 19, ?, 36
Which number is missing?

A	B	C	D	E
29	25	26	28	27

RQ29
   0.5 is to 6 as 12 is to…

A	B	C	D	E
144	36	1	48	96

VQ30
   1/8 is to 2 as ? is to… 16

A	B	C	D	E
2	8	1	1/4	1/5

PART 2: VERBAL ABILITY TEST 3 (30 questions in 9 minutes).

In the questions below, the word outside the bracket will go with only four of the words inside the bracket to make a longer word. Which **one** word will it **not** go with?

VQ1	A	B	C	D	E
out	(stay	strip	do	now	smart)

VQ2	A	B	C	D	E
stop	(page	short	gap	light	watch)

VQ3	A	B	C	D	E
show	(down	room	piece	case	up)

In the questions below, which **one** word has a meaning that extends to or includes the meaning of all the others?

VQ4	A	B	C	D	E
	car	van	lorry	vehicle	bike

VQ5	A	B	C	D	E
	dictionary	book	journal	bible	biography

VQ6	A	B	C	D	E
	clog	brogue	shoe	loafer	moccasin

In the questions below, four of the five sentences have the same meaning. Which **one** sentence has a **different** meaning?

VQ7

A   I shall leave if the weather is fine.
B   The weather was fine so I left.
C   If the weather is fine I can go.
D   My departure requires fine weather.
E   Fine weather is necessary before I can depart.

VQ8

A   The car failed to stop when the lights changed to red.
B   The lights changed to red but the car didn't stop.
C   When the red light came on the car carried on.
D   The car stopped when the lights turned red.
E   The red light came on and the car went through.

VQ9

A   Complete the fitness test before your on-line application.
B   Send your on-line application after completing the fitness test.
C   Submit your application on-line before the fitness test.
D   Complete the fitness test then submit your application on-line.
E   On-line applications should be completed after the fitness test.

VQ10

A   Connect the positive lead first and the negative lead second.
B   Don't connect the negative lead before the positive lead.
C   Connect the negative after first connecting the positive.
D   Only connect the negative after you have connected the positive.
E   Connect the positive after you have connected the negative.

From the five alternatives choose **one** which does not belong with the others.

VQ11					
	A	**B**	**C**	**D**	**E**
	knife	fork	scissors	saw	shears

VQ12					
	A	**B**	**C**	**D**	**E**
	apple	apricot	peach	plum	cherry

VQ13					
	A	**B**	**C**	**D**	**E**
	London	Edinburgh	Cardiff	Belfast	Manchester

In the questions below, the word outside the bracket is similar to **one** of the words inside the bracket. Which **one** word is it similar to?

VQ14					
	A	**B**	**C**	**D**	**E**
agree	(dispute	argue	concur	contradict	reject)

VQ15					
	A	**B**	**C**	**D**	**E**
valid	(mistaken	fallacious	faulty	erroneous	true)

VQ16					
	A	**B**	**C**	**D**	**E**
clumsy	(graceful	elegant	dexterous	unwieldy	adept)

In the questions below, one of the answers goes with both words to make two new words. Which **one** word fits both words?

VQ17				
	A	**B**	**C**	**D**
water..............house	(wheel	fall	front	cress)

VQ18				
	A	**B**	**C**	**D**
paper..............space	(bank	back	weight	less)

VQ19				
	A	**B**	**C**	**D**
thumb..............chair	(arm	screw	wheel	nail)

VQ20				
	A	**B**	**C**	**D**
head..............mind	(stone	rest	board	master)

In the questions below, one of the answers fits with the pair of words inside the bracket. Which **one** word fits the pair?

VQ21				
	A	**B**	**C**	**D**
(straight and true)	honest	correct	hopeful	edge

VQ22				
	A	**B**	**C**	**D**
(desert and leave)	sandy	decline	abandon	barren

VQ23				
	A	**B**	**C**	**D**
(parrot and echo)	mirror	explain	sound	speak

In the questions below, which word or words are missing?

VQ24
The well behaved class were..................begin.

A	B	C	D
already to	all ready too	not already to	all ready to

VQ25
She...................waited for 10 minutes.

A	B	C	D	E
could of	will of	might of	have	should've

VQ26
Success is largely.........................on your interview performance.

A	B	C	D	E
depending	dependant	depends	dependent	dependable

VQ27
.........................no easy answer to sea sickness.

A	B	C	D	E
Theirs	Their's	Thairs	Theres	There's

VQ28
Of all three, Peter's car uses the.........................diesel.

A	B	C	D	E
more	least	fewer	lesser	fewest

The sentences below have a word missing. Which **one** word makes the best sense of the sentence.

VQ29

Employers want people who will add...................to their business and not detract from it.

A	B	C	D	E
meaning	knowledge	value	integrity	experience

VQ30

Although he had missed the tutorial, the student could still write a good essay if he was able to glean the...................information from his colleagues.

A	B	C	D	E
useful	helpful	valuable	precise	relevant

PART 3: NUMERACY TEST 3 (30 questions in 16 minutes).

NQ1   298 – 89 =

A	B	C	D	E
209	219	208	199	198

NQ2   What is 85 pence expressed as a fraction of £1?

A	B	C	D	E
9/10	17/20	18/20	17/25	47/50

NQ3   The circumference of the earth is 24859.82 miles. What is this distance correct to two significant figures?

A	B	C	D	E
24859.82	24000	25000	24800	24900

NQ4   A cube has a volume of 8 cm^3. In cm^2, the surface area of the cube is:

A	B	C	D	E
16	48	32	24	40

NQ5   What is 33 x 11?

A	B	C	D	E
363	333	366	336	343

NQ6 A pupil scored 55% in a test. If the maximum possible mark was 200, then the pupil's mark was:

A	B	C	D	E
100	110	105	155	95

NQ7 If $x = 3/4$ and $y = 2/3$ then $x - y =$

A	B	C	D	E
1/12	1/6	1/8	1/10	1/9

NQ8 $\dfrac{2}{3} \div \dfrac{1}{4} =$

A	B	C	D	E
$2\dfrac{2}{5}$	$2\dfrac{3}{4}$	$2\dfrac{1}{2}$	$2\dfrac{1}{3}$	$2\dfrac{2}{3}$

NQ9 If the small (hour) hand of a clock turns by 5 hours, through how many degrees has it turned?

A	B	C	D	E
135	180	240	150	140

NQ10 One nautical mile = 1.15077945 miles.
What distance is this correct to two significant figures?

A	B	C	D	E
1.1	1.15	1.0	1.151	1.2

NQ11   1750 x 0.002 =

A	B	C	D	E
35	350	3500	3.5	0.35

NQ12   Which of the following numbers is the largest?

A	B	C	D	E
2.255	2.26	2.259	2.2	2.199

NQ13   What is 3/8 expressed as a decimal?

A	B	C	D	E
0.373	0.38	0.375	0.372	0.33

NQ14   What is 3.14159 corrected to three decimal places?

A	B	C	D	E
3.1416	3.142	3.1425	3.14	3.145

NQ15   The area of a square is 900 cm^2. What is its perimeter in cm?

A	B	C	D	E
300	30	180	120	90

NQ16   What is 625 ÷ 25?

A	B	C	D	E
18	20	25	26	24

NQ17 How many school periods lasting 35 minutes each can fit into five hours of lesson time?

A	B	C	D	E
8	6	7	9	5

NQ18 If $v = 10$ and $u = 7.5$ then $v(v - u) =$

A	B	C	D	E
75	2.5	25	7.5	92.5

NQ19 $1\frac{1}{4} \times 90 =$

A	B	C	D	E
108	112.5	110	116.5	114.5

NQ20 If the small (hour) hand of a clock turns by 8 hours, through how many degrees has it turned?

A	B	C	D	E
270	135	90	360	240

NQ21 0.04896 rounded to three significant figures is:

A	B	C	D	E
0.0500	0.048	0.489	0.049	0.500

NQ22 14499 rounded to the nearest ten is:

A	B	C	D	E
14000	14090	15000	14590	14500

NQ23 A diesel engine burns air and fuel in the ratio 14.5 to 1. How many grams of air are burned with 8 grams of fuel?

A	B	C	D	E
145	120	116	125	118

NQ24 75.54% as a decimal to one decimal place is:

A	B	C	D	E
0.8	0.75	0.76	0.755	0.7

NQ25 What is the perimeter of the following shape in cm?

12 cm

A	B	C	D	E
84	60	48	68	72

NQ26 What is the highest common factor of 8 and 20?

A	B	C	D	E
8	20	2	4	5

NQ27　$5\frac{1}{2} \div 3 =$

A	B	C	D	E
$2\frac{1}{3}$	$1\frac{5}{6}$	$1\frac{1}{3}$	$1\frac{1}{6}$	$1\frac{2}{3}$

NQ28　If 1 kilometre = 0.621371192 miles, how many miles is 10000 kilometres to the nearest mile?

A	B	C	D	E
6213	6200	6214	6217	6210

NQ29　If the minute (large) hand of a clock makes 6 complete revolutions, by how many degrees does it turn through?

A	B	C	D	E
2160	2240	2400	1800	2100

NQ30　If the hour (small) hand of a clock turns through 30 minutes, by how many degrees does it turn through?

A	B	C	D	E
30^0	12^0	24^0	10^0	15^0

PART 4: MECHANICAL TEST 3 (30 questions in 10 minutes).

MQ1   Which of these three shapes has the largest area? (if all the same, mark D).

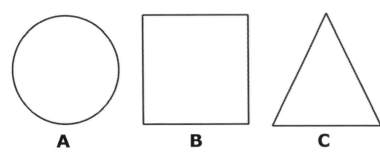

A   **B**   **C**   **D**

MQ2   If the end of the rope is pulled upwards by one metre then the the weight will be raised by:

A 20 cm
B 25 cm
C 50 cm
D 1.5 m

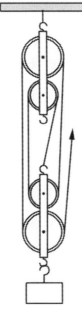

MQ3 In the electrical equation V = IR, what are the units of I?

A Volts
B Ohms
C Watts
D Amps

MQ4 In this system of gears which gear is rotating at the slowest
speed (mark D, if impossible to tell).

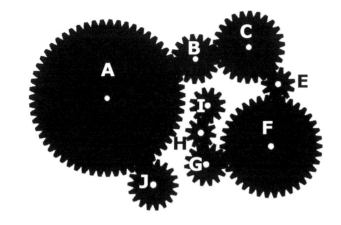

A B C D E F G H I J

MQ5   In diagrams of electrical circuits the symbol below is used to
represent:

A a variable resistor
B a lamp or bulb
C a light emitting diode
D a negative lead

MQ6 Three balls are placed at different heights on a child's slide and
released. Which ball takes the longest time from leaving the end
of the slide to hitting the ground? (if all the same, mark D).

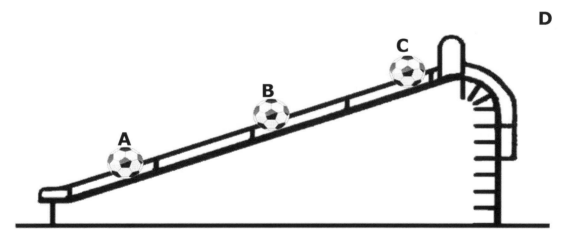

MQ7 Which of these objects is in a state of static equilibrium?

A apple
B pencil
C spoon
D all three

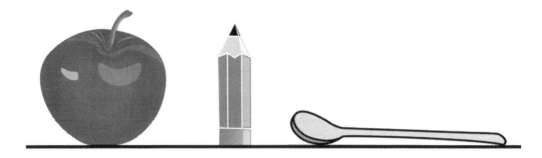

MQ8 What is the mechanical advantage of these chain-linked bicycle gears?

A 1
B less than 1
C more than 1
D impossible to say

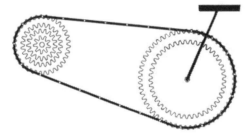

MQ9 When removing a screw, which of these screwdrivers provides the highest mechanical advantage? (if all the same, mark D).

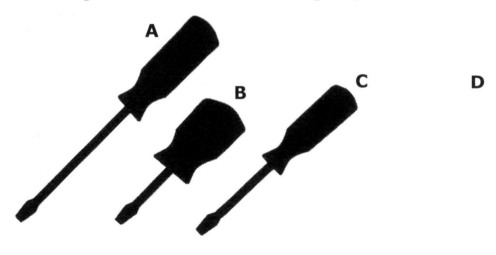

MQ10 How many bulbs are lit in this circuit?

A 0
B 1
C 2
D 3

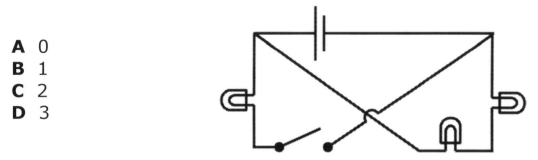

MQ11 Which of these book shelves can support the most weight? (if all the same, mark D)

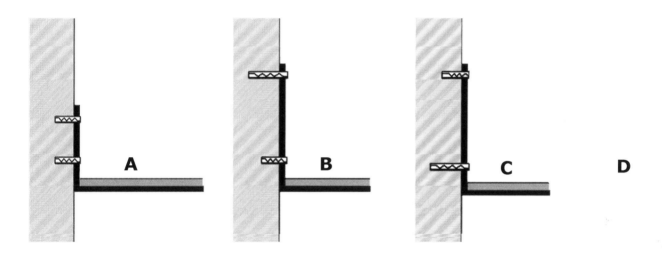

MQ12 Which concrete block is the easiest to lift off the ground? (if all the same, mark D).

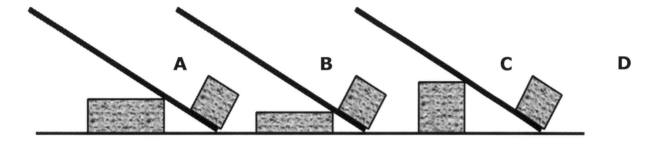

MQ13 Which of these handwheels has the highest mechanical
       advantage? (if all the same, mark D).

D

MQ14 What temperature is this thermometer reading?

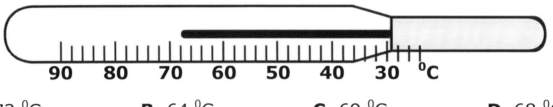

A 72 ^{0}C   **B** 64 ^{0}C   **C** 69 ^{0}C   **D** 68 ^{0}C

MQ15 These bulbs and resistors are connected in:

A series only
B parallel only
C both series and parallel
D neither series nor parallel

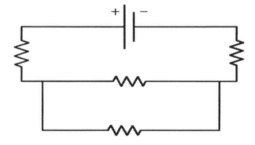

MQ16 When the pendulum is released, at what position is the tension
      'T' in the rope at its highest? (if all the same, mark D).

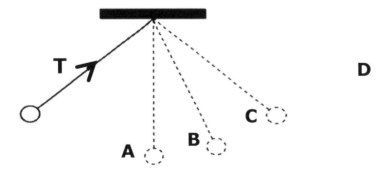

D

138

MQ17 Where would you place the load in this wheelbarrow to achieve the best mechanical advantage? (if all the same, mark D).

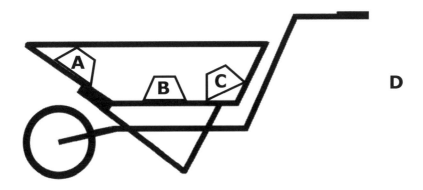

D

MQ18 Which belt wheels are turning anti-clockwise?

A A,B,C, and G
B F, D and E
C A and B
D F and D

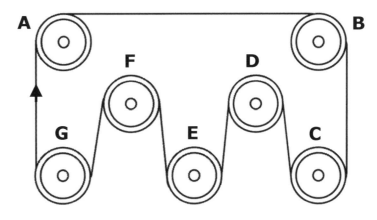

MQ19 What is the force 'F' in kilograms applied to the pulley rope?

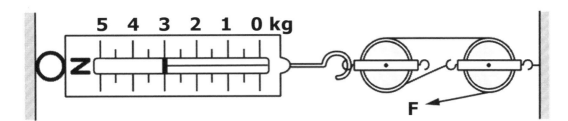

A 3 kg
B 2 kg
C 1.5 kg
D 6 kg

MQ20   Which of these three floating blocks is made from the most
       dense material? (mark D if impossible to say).

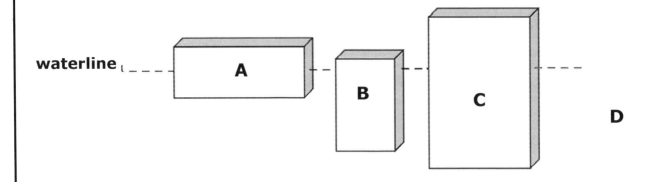

MQ21   What is the maximum output current of this transformer?

A 5 A
B 0.5 A
C 10 A
D 50 A

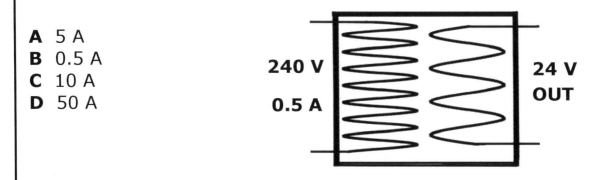

MQ22   At which angle will the football travel the farthest distance? (if
       all the same, mark D).

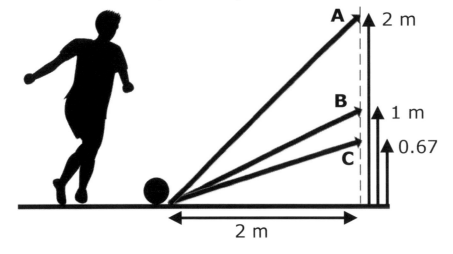

MQ23 A spring extends by 5 cm when a 1 kg weight is attached.
By how many centimetres will the spring extend by when
an additional 4 kg is attached?

A 20 cm
B 30 cm
C 15 cm
D 25 cm

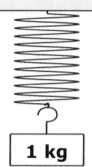

MQ24 If you close the switch, which bulb will be the dimmest?
(if all the same, mark D).

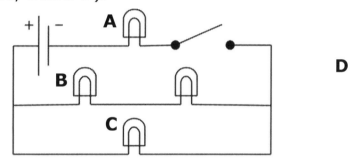

MQ25 Which pendulum swings the slowest? (if all the same, mark D).

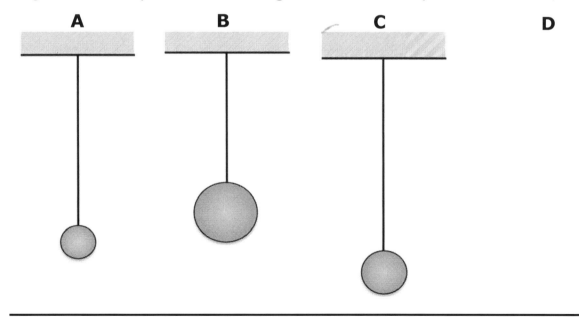

MQ26 Which of these levers is not a force multiplier? (mark D if none).

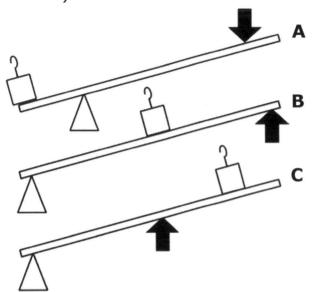

MQ27 If the larger cog spins at 600 rpm, how quickly does the smaller cog spin?

A 600 rpm
B 450 rpm
C 720 rpm
D 800 rpm

MQ28 Which crane has the heaviest counterweight? (if all the same, mark D).

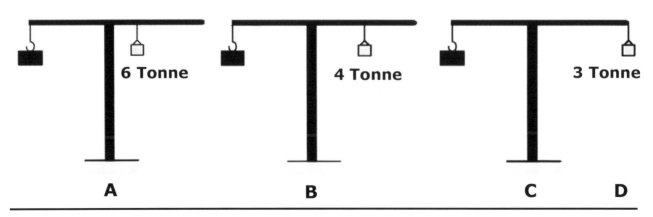

6 Tonne   4 Tonne   3 Tonne

A   B   C   D

MQ29   Which bulbs will not light because they have been dangerously
'shorted-out' by the thick wire?

A   B2 and B3
B   B1 and B2
C   B1 and B2
D   all three

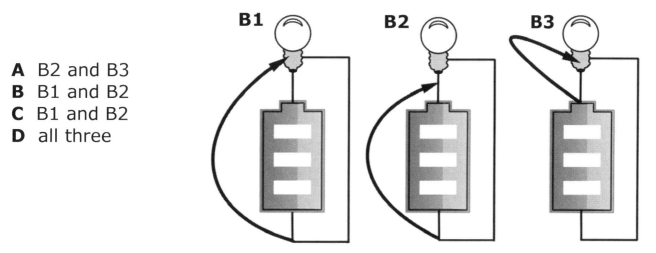

MQ30   Which lever lifts the weight with the least effort? (if all the
same, mark D).

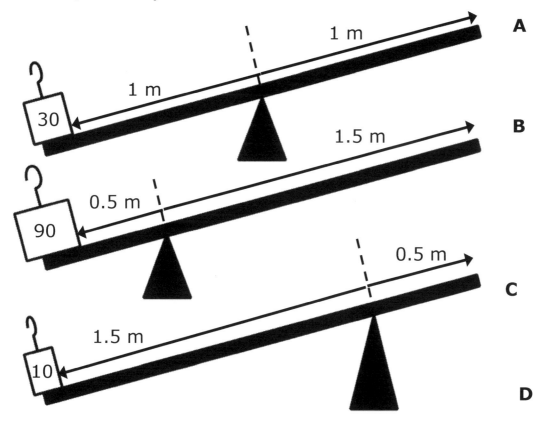

PRACTICE TEST 4

Part 1: Reasoning

Part 2: Verbal Ability

Part 3: Numerical

Part 4: Mechanical

PART 1: REASONING TEST 4 (30 questions in 9 minutes).

RQ1   OPPORTUNE means the same as...

A	B	C	D	E
FORTUNATE	POSSIBLE	RISKY	FAVOURITE	SEASONAL

RQ2   LIMITED is the opposite of...

A	B	C	D	E
SUFFICIENT	INFINITE	NARROW	FIXED	RESTRICTED

RQ3   SUGAR is to CARBOHYDRATE as AMINO ACID is to...

A	B	C	D	E
MEAT	EGGS	PROTEIN	FISH	FRUIT

RQ4

Which of the following boxes of shapes is the odd one out?

A	B	C	D	E

RQ5   Consider the following shape:

Which of the following shapes is a rotation of the shape above?

A	B	C	D	E

146

RQ6   Consider this sequence of diagrams:

Which of the following comes next?

A	**B**	**C**	**D**	**E**

RQ7 Consider this sequence of numbers: 99, 88, 78, 69, 61...
Which of the following comes next?

A	**B**	**C**	**D**	**E**
52	53	54	56	55

R

Q8 Consider this sequence of numbers: 576, 288, 96, 48, 16...
Which of the following comes next?

A	**B**	**C**	**D**	**E**
2	6	4	8	12

RQ9

10 is to 2 as ? is to 3

A	**B**	**C**	**D**	**E**
12	15	20	30	9

RQ10

1.5 is to 30 as 1/8 is to...

A	**B**	**C**	**D**	**E**
2	3.2	2.5	3.125	2.25

RQ11   INFALLIBLE means the same as...

A	B	C	D	E
UNRELIABLE	STEADY	IMPERFECT	ERRANT	FOOLPROOF

RQ12   PRECEDENT is the opposite of ...

A	B	C	D	E
PRIOR	SOONER	PREVIOUS	LATER	FORMER

RQ13   ACCIDENT is to CATASTROPHE as LUCK is to...

A	B	C	D	E
WINDFALL	CHANCE	DISASTER	MISHAP	RESULT

RQ14

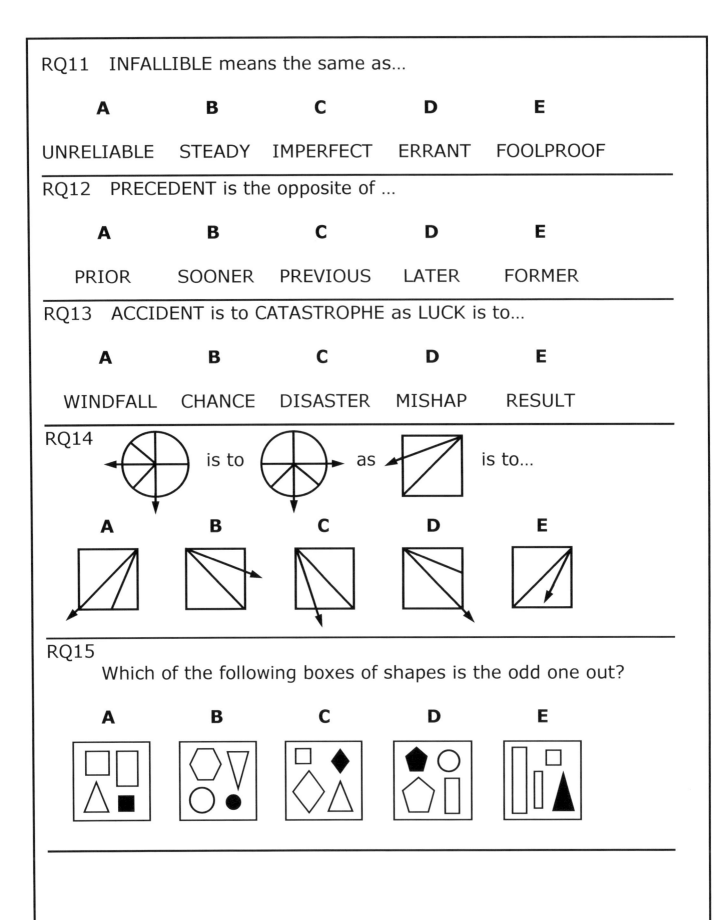

is to ... as ... is to...

A   B   C   D   E

RQ15

Which of the following boxes of shapes is the odd one out?

A   B   C   D   E

RQ16   Consider this sequence of shapes:

Which of the following comes next?

A	B	C	D	E

R

Q17   Consider this sequence of numbers: 5, 11, 23, 47...
Which of the following comes next?

A	B	C	D	E
85	87	94	95	93

R

Q18   Consider this sequence of numbers: 1, 9, 2, 8, 3, 7, 4, 6, 5...
Which of the following comes next?

A	B	C	D	E
4	6	5	3	7

R

Q19

8 is to 2 as 2 is to...

A	B	C	D	E
4	1	1/8	1/2	1/4

RQ20

$2x$ is to $5y$ as $6x$ is to...

A	B	C	D	E
30y	15x	30x	15xy	15y

RQ21   DISARRAY means the same as...

A	B	C	D	E
PARADE	CHAOS	DEBILITATE	ORDER	DISPLAY

RQ22   OMIT is the opposite of ...

A	B	C	D	E
INCLUDE	IGNORE	DELETE	BYPASS	SKIP

RQ23   MONEY is to PROSPERITY as JOB is to...

A	B	C	D	E
EMPLOYMENT	WORK	WEALTH	FUTURE	CAREER

RQ24

Which shape is identical to this shape?

A   B   C   D

RQ25

is to ... as ... is to...

A   B   C   D   E

RQ26   Consider this sequence:

Which of the following fills the missing space?

A	B	C	D	E
T	V	Y	E	A

RQ27   Consider this sequence of numbers: 1, 1, 2, 6, 24...
Which of the following comes next?

A	B	C	D	E
72	112	120	48	96

R

Q28   Consider this sequence of numbers: 32, 29, 30, 27, 28, 25
Which of the following comes next?

A	B	C	D	E
26	23	24	31	33

RQ29
    9 is to 8 as 72 is to...

A	B	C	D	E
80	68	36	64	48

RQ30
    4 is to 1 as ? is to 16

A	B	C	D	E
4	64	48	2	56

PART 2: VERBAL ABILITY TEST 4 (30 questions in 9 minutes).

In the questions below, the word outside the bracket will go with only four of the words inside the bracket to make a longer word. Which **one** word will it **not** go with?

	A	B	C	D	E
VQ1					
ten (men	able	fold	pin	ant)

	A	B	C	D	E
VQ2					
pin (hole	number	ion	point	stripe)

	A	B	C	D	E
VQ3					
hand (hold	made	written	shake	chosen)

In the questions below, which **one** word has a meaning that extends to or includes the meaning of all the others?

	A	B	C	D	E
VQ4					
	boat	tug	ferry	tanker	barge

	A	B	C	D	E
VQ5					
	shower	rainfall	thunderstorm	snow	precipitation

	A	B	C	D	E
VQ6					
	tea	coffee	drink	water	juice

In the questions below, four of the five sentences have the same meaning. Which **one** sentence has a **different** meaning?

VQ7

A I go home only at the weekend.
B I only go home at the weekend.
C The weekend is the only time I go home.
D Only I go home at the weekend.
E I go home at the weekend only.

VQ8

A Like him, I don't understand it.
B I don't understand it like he does.
C Neither of us understand it.
D I, like him, don't understand it.
E Neither he nor I understand it.

VQ9

A The offer of a work placement is open to everyone.
B Work placements are not available for everyone.
C Not everyone will be offered a work placement.
D There isn't a work placement available for you all.
E A work placement is not guaranteed for all people.

VQ10

A The message is lost when important details are omitted.
B Miss out salient details and the message is lost.
C It important not to miss the details in the message.
D Remember the important details or lose the message.
E Don't lose the message by missing out salient details.

In the questions below, the sentence has a word missing. Which **one** word makes the best sense of the sentence?

VQ11
There was insufficient information to make an........................decision.

A	B	C	D	E
executive	informal	early	informed	sensible

VQ12
Applicants need to identify their strengths and skill.....................

A	B	C	D	E
shortages	problems	detriments	defects	deficiencies

From the five alternatives choose **one** word which does not belong with the others.

VQ13

A	B	C	D	E
smell	size	taste	sight	touch

VQ14

A	B	C	D	E
chair	pew	couch	bed	settee

VQ15

A	B	C	D	E
pen	pencil	ruler	crayon	chalk

In the questions below, the word outside the bracket is similar to **one** of the words inside the bracket. Which **one** word is it similar to?

VQ16

	A	B	C	D	E
inept	(clumsy	dangerous	skilful	careful	stupid)

VQ17

	A	B	C	D	E
precursor	(proceed	latterly	next	precede	shortly)

VQ18

	A	B	C	D	E
protocol	(plans	rules	steps	codes	actions)

In the questions below, one of the answers goes with both words to make two new words. Which **one** word fits both words?

VQ19

	A	B	C	D
road..............hops	(runner	block	works	side)

VQ20

	A	B	C	D
door..............gap	(post	stop	year	frame)

VQ21

	A	B	C	D
play..............sheet	(bed	group	work	ground)

VQ22

	A	B	C	D
song..............song	(bird	book	sheet	sing)

In the questions below, one of the answers fits with the pair of words inside the bracket. Which **one** word fits the pair?

VQ23	**A**	**B**	**C**	**D**
(knife and fork)	spoon	cup	saucer	cutlery

VQ24	**A**	**B**	**C**	**D**
(store and keep)	shed	renew	retain	dispose

VQ25	**A**	**B**	**C**	**D**
(degree and area)	course	extent	first	size

In the questions below, the sentence has a word missing. Which **one** word makes the best sense of the sentence?

VQ26
The driver had planned his journey in advance to minimise hold-ups which lengthen the time on the road and increase the.........................of tiredness and frustration.

A	**B**	**C**	**D**	**E**
frequency	speed	amount	likelihood	feelings

VQ27
An officer from the Antiques Squad spotted some.........................looking artefacts in the window of a local antique dealer.

A	**B**	**C**	**D**	**E**
familiar	interesting	ancient	pleasant	useful

In the questions below, the sentence has a word missing. Which **one** word makes the best sense of the sentence?

VQ28

Charges for long-term parking at airports are chosen to.......................... a stay of at least four hours.

A	B	C	D	E
ensure	allow	promote	permit	encourage

VQ29

Mike's poor performance was.................to the team as a whole.

A	B	C	D	E
difficult	problematic	detrimental	beneficial	unfortunate

VQ30

A sick child can.................a parent's daily routine.

A	B	C	D	E
influence	disrupt	modify	damage	determine

PART 3: NUMERACY TEST 4 (30 questions in 16 minutes).

NQ1   80 x 250 =

A	B	C	D	E
2000	8000	1000	10000	20000

NQ2   The percentage increase in speed from 25 mph to 30 mph is:

A	B	C	D	E
5%	20%	10%	25%	15%

NQ3   The area of the UK is 243610 km². What is the area written to three significant figures?

A	B	C	D	E
244000	240000	243000	243	243600

NQ4   A rectangular field of length 100 metres is four times as long as it is broad. The perimeter of the field in metres is:

A	B	C	D	E
150	300	250	225	400

NQ5   What is 32 x 120?

A	B	C	D	E
3800	3620	3840	3760	3480

NQ6 A candidate scored 64 out of 80 in a test. What was the mark as a percentage?

A	B	C	D	E
70	72	80	82	66

NQ7 If $x = 18$ and $y = 95$ then $y - 2x =$

A	B	C	D	E
57	59	60	63	77

NQ8 $2\frac{3}{4} + 1\frac{1}{2} =$

A	B	C	D	E
$3\frac{3}{4}$	$4\frac{1}{2}$	$3\frac{1}{4}$	$4\frac{1}{4}$	$4\frac{5}{6}$

NQ9 If the large (minute) hand of a clock turns by 55 minutes, through how many degrees has it turned?

A	B	C	D	E
348	326	348	332	330

NQ10 The distance from the Earth to the Moon is 384400 km. What distance is this rounded to the nearest 1000 km?

A	B	C	D	E
384000	385000	380000	300000	384400

NQ11   4440 x 0.002 =

A	B	C	D	E
880	88	0.88	8.88	8.9

NQ12   A rectangular fish tank holds 50 litres of water when filled to the top. How deep is the tank in centimetres if the base measures 40 cm by 50 cm.

A	B	C	D	E
40	48	60	50	25

NQ13   What is 32/40 expressed as a decimal?

A	B	C	D	E
0.64	0.8	0.76	0.72	0.75

NQ14   1 litre = 0.219969157 Imperial gallons. What is this number to four decimal places?

A	B	C	D	E
0.21996	0.21997	0.2100	0.2190	0.2200

NQ15   The perimeter of a square playing field is 1200 metres. What is its area in m^2?

A	B	C	D	E
9000	300	90000	30000	900000

NQ16 What is 170 ÷ 2.5?

A	B	C	D	E
68	51	58	65	66

NQ17 How many plant pots costing 75p each can be bought for £10?

A	B	C	D	E
12	13	11	15	14

NQ18 If $p = 72$ and $r = 50$ then $r(p - r) =$

A	B	C	D	E
1050	1150	1100	72	1200

NQ19 $1\frac{3}{4} \div 2\frac{1}{2} =$

A	B	C	D	E
$\frac{1}{2}$	$\frac{3}{5}$	$\frac{5}{9}$	$\frac{7}{10}$	$\frac{5}{8}$

NQ20 If the large (minute) hand of a clock turns by 1 minute, through how many degrees has it turned?

A	B	C	D	E
12	5	10	4	6

NQ21 Which of the following numbers is the smallest?

A	B	C	D	E
1.375	1.359	1.33	1.369	1.34

NQ22 $40000 \times 6.25 =$

A	B	C	D	E
256250	241000	251000	250000	25000

NQ23 A wallet contains £50 of which 20% is in coins, and the rest in five pound notes. How many five pound notes are there?

A	B	C	D	E
5	4	3	7	8

NQ24 87.5 % as a decimal to one decimal places is:

A	B	C	D	E
0.87	0.88	0.8	0.9	88

NQ25 What is the length 'x' if the area of the rectangle is 44 cm^2?

8 cm

x cm

A	B	C	D	E
5.5	6.5	6	5.75	4.5

NQ26 $45 \times \dfrac{8}{9} =$

A	B	C	D	E
38	40	44	36	42

NQ27   What is the highest common factor of 88 and 44?

A	B	C	D	E
11	22	2	44	4

NQ28   80% as a fraction in its lowest terms is:

A	B	C	D	E
$\dfrac{2}{5}$	$\dfrac{4}{5}$	$\dfrac{16}{20}$	$\dfrac{8}{10}$	$\dfrac{20}{25}$

NQ29   If the hour (small) hand of a clock moves from 2 pm to 10 pm, by how many degrees does it turn through?

A	B	C	D	E
180^0	270^0	120^0	60^0	240^0

NQ30   If the minute (large) hand of a clock turns from 10.00 hours to 10.20 hours by how many degrees does it turn through?

A	B	C	D	E
120^0	30^0	150^0	180^0	90^0

PART 4: MECHANICAL TEST 4 (30 questions in 10 minutes).

MQ1 In this electrical circuit, what is the voltage across the bulb if the voltmeter reads 3 volts across the resistor?

A 3 V
B 6 V
C 9 V
D 12 V

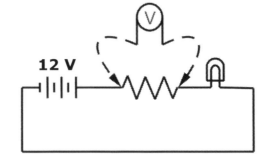

MQ2 If the levers are the same length, which one lifts the load the with the least effort? (if all the same, mark D)

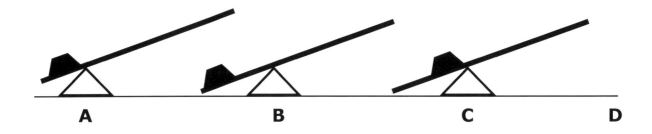

A   **B**   **C**   **D**

MQ3 At what position would you need to place the fulcrum to balance the bar?

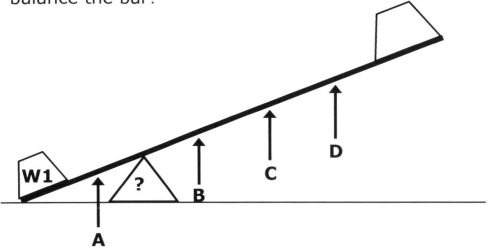

MQ4　Which pulley uses the least effort to lift a 100 kg weight off the ground to the height of the platform? (if all the same, mark D).

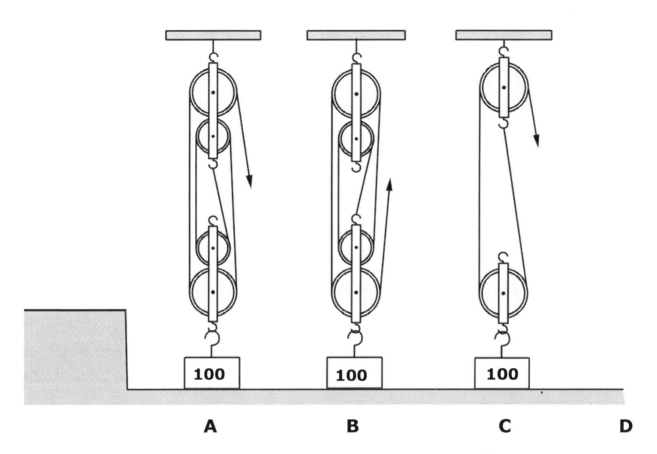

A　　　　　**B**　　　　　**C**　　　　　**D**

MQ5　It takes 'gear 1' ten seconds to complete one revolution. How fast is 'gear 2' turning?

A　6 rpm
B　7 rpm
C　8 rpm
D　9 rpm

MQ6 If the top rack moves to the left at a constant speed, how does the bottom rack move?

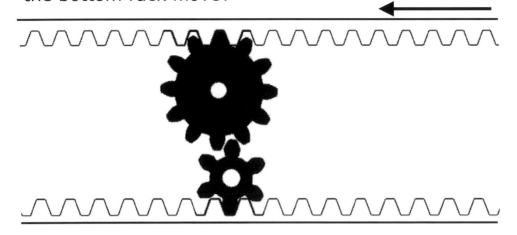

A   To the right at the same speed
B   To the left at twice the speed
C   To the left at the same speed
D   To the right at twice the speed

MQ7 How many switches need to be closed to light three bulbs?

A 2
B 3
C 4
D 5

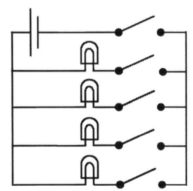

MQ8 In diagrams of electrical circuits the symbol below is used to represent:

A a capacitor
B a light emitting diode
C a resistor
D a variable resistor

MQ9 Which of the three ship hulls is most likely to capsize if 'G' marks the centre of mass? (if all the same mark D)

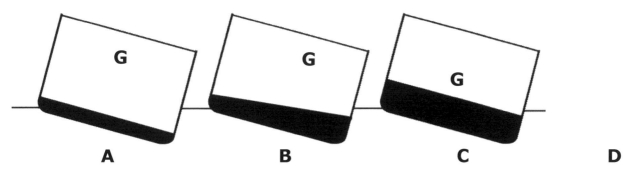

A   B   C   D

MQ10   How heavy is 'W' if the scales are balanced?

A 5 g
B 10 g
C 15 g
D 7.5 g

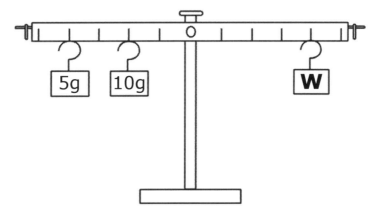

MQ11 Which car is about to topple over if 'X' marks its centre of gravity (if impossible to tell, mark D).

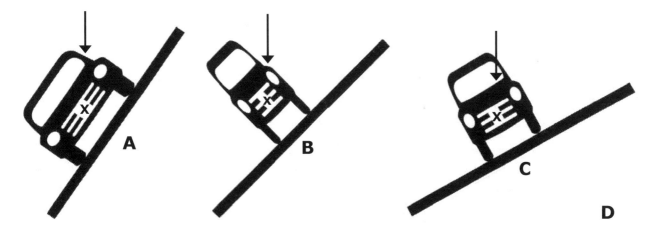

A   B   C   D

MQ12 These three flywheels are of equal weight and spinning at the same speed. Which flywheel will take the longest time to stop? (if all the same, mark D).

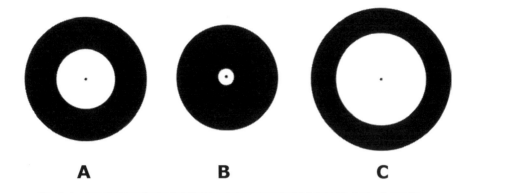

| A | B | C | D |

MQ13 The three fans are rotating at the same number of revolutions per minute. Which fan has the highest speed at its tip? (if all the same mark D)

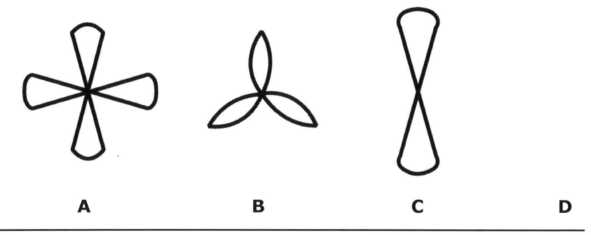

| A | B | C | D |

MQ14 Which of these three floating blocks is the heaviest? (mark D if impossible to say).

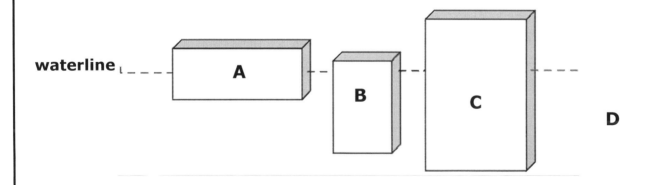

MQ15 In these circuits, which bulbs will light up?

A 1, 2 and 3
B Only 1 and 3
C Only 2
D No bulbs lit

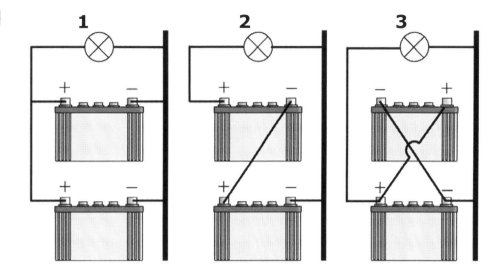

MQ16 In diagrams of electrical circuits the symbol below is used to represent:

A a fuse
B a resistor
C a diode
D a capacitor

MQ17 Who is the lightest person standing on the end of the lever?

A Alan - 75 kg
B Brian - 72 kg
C Chloe - 64 kg
D David - 79 kg

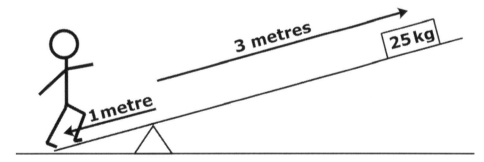

MQ18 These three 12 volt bulbs are identical and require at least
       6 volts to light. When the switch is closed:

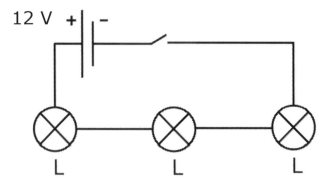

A all the bulbs light up fully
B all the bulbs light up dimly
C only one bulb lights up
D no bulbs light up

MQ19 These four 12 volt bulbs are identical and require at least
       6 volts to light.   How many bulbs are lit up?

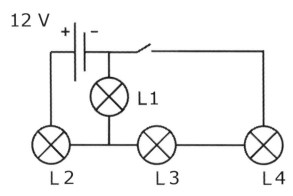

A only L1 and L2 are lit
B only L2, L3 and L4 are lit
C all the bulbs are lit
D no bulbs are lit

MQ20 Which of these pulley systems does not reduce the force needed
       to lift the weight?

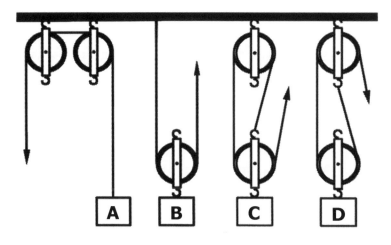

MQ21 Which rollers are turning clockwise?

A 1, 2, 5 and 6
B 1, 2, 3 and 4
C 1, 2, 4 and 5
D 3, 4 and 5

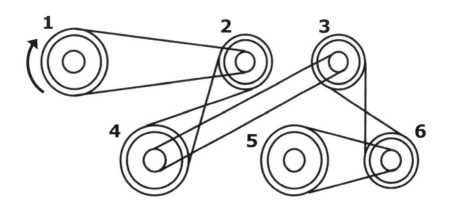

MQ22 How heavy is the weight 'W' in kilograms?

A 1 kg
B 2 kg
C 3 kg
D 4 kg

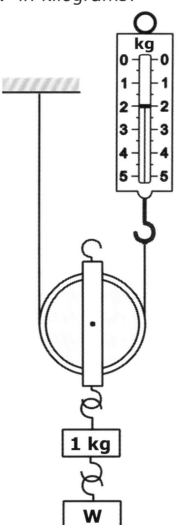

MQ23 Which tank generates the highest static water pressure at the outlet? (if all the same mark D).

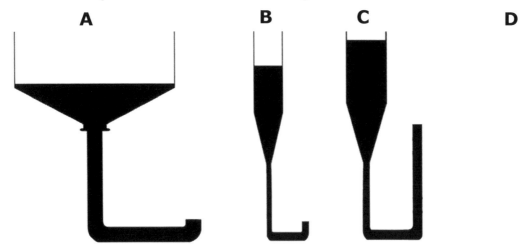

MQ24 These three steel balls are released at the same time from the same position on three identical ramps.   Which steel ball will reach the end of its ramp first? (if all the same mark D).

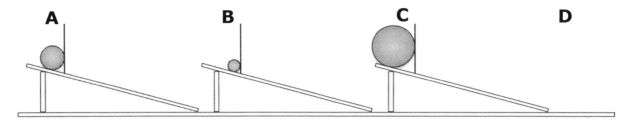

MQ25 Which of these cones is not in a state of stable equilibrium?

A C2 only
B C3 only
C C2 and C3
D all three

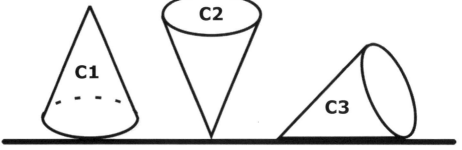

MQ26 If the top bulb is removed, how many bulbs will remain lit?

A 2 bulbs
B 3 bulbs
C 4 bulbs
D None

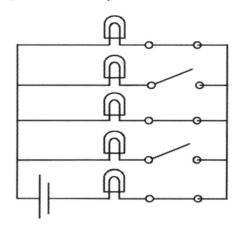

MQ27 Which siphon will empty the fluid in the upper jar the most quickly? (if all the same mark D).

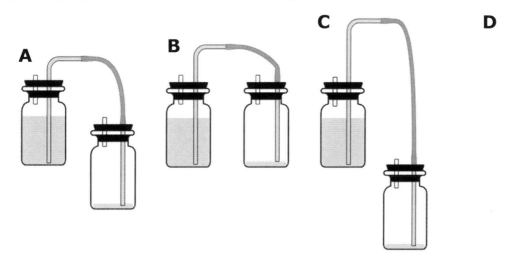

MQ28 In which direction should this aircraft take off if there is a south-westerly wind blowing?

A south-west
B north-west
C south-east
D south-west

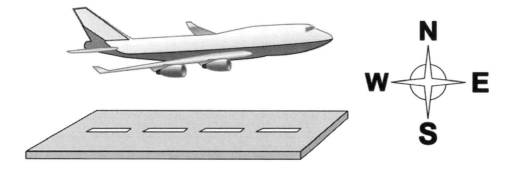

MQ29 Which pulley system is not in equilibrium? (if none, mark D).

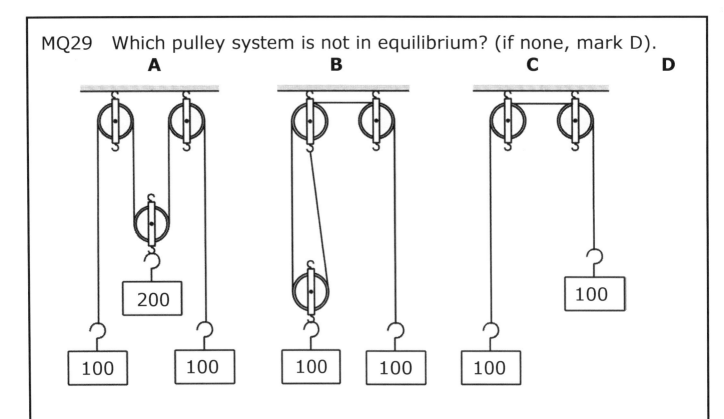

MQ30 Which of these identical cargo ships is carrying the heaviest load if all three ships are afloat? (if impossible to say, mark D).

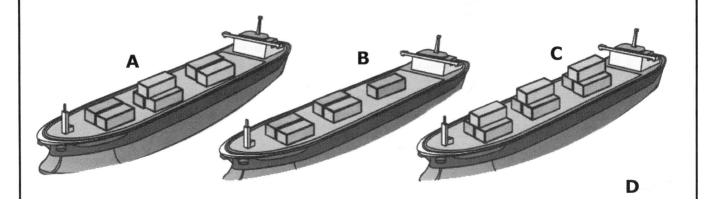

ANSWER RECORD SHEETS

(Expanded answers follow on)

Answer Record Sheet: TEST 1

Reasoning

RQ1	A	B	<u>C</u>	D	E
RQ2	A	B	C	<u>D</u>	E
RQ3	A	B	C	D	<u>E</u>
RQ4	A	B	<u>C</u>	D	E
RQ5	A	B	C	<u>D</u>	E
RQ6	A	<u>B</u>	C	D	E
RQ7	A	B	C	<u>D</u>	E
RQ8	<u>A</u>	B	C	D	E
RQ9	A	B	C	<u>D</u>	E
RQ10	<u>A</u>	B	C	D	E
RQ11	A	<u>B</u>	C	D	E
RQ12	A	B	<u>C</u>	D	E
RQ13	A	B	C	D	<u>E</u>
RQ14	A	B	C	<u>D</u>	E
RQ15	A	B	C	D	<u>E</u>
RQ16	A	B	<u>C</u>	D	E
RQ17	<u>A</u>	B	C	D	E
RQ18	A	<u>B</u>	C	D	E
RQ19	A	B	<u>C</u>	D	E
RQ20	A	B	C	D	<u>E</u>
RQ21	A	<u>B</u>	C	D	E
RQ22	<u>A</u>	B	C	D	E
RQ23	A	B	C	<u>D</u>	E
RQ24	A	B	<u>C</u>	D	E
RQ25	A	<u>B</u>	C	D	E
RQ26	<u>A</u>	B	C	D	E
RQ27	A	B	C	<u>D</u>	E
RQ28	A	B	C	D	<u>E</u>
RQ29	A	<u>B</u>	C	D	E
RQ30	A	B	C	D	<u>E</u>

Verbal Ability

VQ1	A	B	<u>C</u>	D	E
VQ2	A	B	C	<u>D</u>	E
VQ3	A	B	C	D	<u>E</u>
VQ4	<u>A</u>	B	C	D	E
VQ5	A	<u>B</u>	C	D	E
VQ6	A	B	C	D	<u>E</u>
VQ7	A	B	<u>C</u>	D	E
VQ8	A	B	C	D	<u>E</u>
VQ9	A	B	C	<u>D</u>	E
VQ10	<u>A</u>	B	C	D	E
VQ11	A	<u>B</u>	C	D	E
VQ12	A	B	C	<u>D</u>	E
VQ13	A	B	<u>C</u>	D	E
VQ14	A	B	C	D	<u>E</u>
VQ15	A	<u>B</u>	C	D	E
VQ16	A	B	<u>C</u>	D	E
VQ17	A	B	<u>C</u>	D	E
VQ18	<u>A</u>	B	C	D	E
VQ19	A	B	<u>C</u>	D	E
VQ20	A	<u>B</u>	C	D	E
VQ21	A	B	C	<u>D</u>	E
VQ22	A	<u>B</u>	C	D	E
VQ23	<u>A</u>	B	C	D	E
VQ24	A	B	C	D	<u>E</u>
VQ25	A	<u>B</u>	C	D	E
VQ26	A	B	C	<u>D</u>	E
VQ27	A	B	C	D	<u>E</u>
VQ28	A	B	<u>C</u>	D	E
VQ29	<u>A</u>	B	C	D	E
VQ30	A	B	C	<u>D</u>	E

Answer Record Sheet: TEST 1

Numerical Reasoning

NQ1	A	B	C	D	<u>E</u>
NQ2	A	<u>B</u>	C	D	E
NQ3	<u>A</u>	B	C	D	E
NQ4	A	B	<u>C</u>	D	E
NQ5	A	<u>B</u>	C	D	E
NQ6	A	B	C	D	<u>E</u>
NQ7	A	B	C	<u>D</u>	E
NQ8	<u>A</u>	B	C	D	E
NQ9	A	B	C	D	<u>E</u>
NQ10	<u>A</u>	B	C	D	E
NQ11	A	B	<u>C</u>	D	E
NQ12	A	B	<u>C</u>	D	E
NQ13	A	B	C	<u>D</u>	E
NQ14	A	<u>B</u>	C	D	E
NQ15	A	B	<u>C</u>	D	E
NQ16	<u>A</u>	B	C	D	E
NQ17	A	B	C	<u>D</u>	E
NQ18	A	<u>B</u>	C	D	E
NQ19	<u>A</u>	B	C	D	E
NQ20	A	B	C	<u>D</u>	E
NQ21	A	B	C	D	<u>E</u>
NQ22	A	<u>B</u>	C	D	E
NQ23	A	B	C	<u>D</u>	E
NQ24	A	B	<u>C</u>	D	E
NQ25	A	B	C	D	<u>E</u>
NQ26	<u>A</u>	B	C	D	E
NQ27	<u>A</u>	B	C	D	E
NQ28	A	B	<u>C</u>	D	E
NQ29	A	<u>B</u>	C	D	E
NQ30	A	B	C	<u>D</u>	E

Mechanical Comprehension

MQ1	A	<u>B</u>	C	D
MQ2	A	B	<u>C</u>	D
MQ3	<u>A</u>	B	C	D
MQ4	A	B	<u>C</u>	D
MQ5	A	<u>B</u>	C	D
MQ6	A	B	C	<u>D</u>
MQ7	A	B	<u>C</u>	D
MQ8	<u>A</u>	B	C	D
MQ9	A	B	C	<u>D</u>
MQ10	A	B	<u>C</u>	D
MQ11	<u>A</u>	B	C	D
MQ12	A	<u>B</u>	C	D
MQ13	A	B	<u>C</u>	D
MQ14	A	<u>B</u>	C	D
MQ15	A	B	C	<u>D</u>
MQ16	<u>A</u>	B	C	D
MQ17	A	B	C	<u>D</u>
MQ18	A	<u>B</u>	C	D
MQ19	A	B	<u>C</u>	D
MQ20	A	B	<u>C</u>	D
MQ21	<u>A</u>	B	C	D
MQ22	A	<u>B</u>	C	D
MQ23	<u>A</u>	B	C	D
MQ24	A	B	C	<u>D</u>
MQ25	<u>A</u>	B	C	D
MQ26	A	<u>B</u>	C	D
MQ27	A	B	<u>C</u>	D
MQ28	A	<u>B</u>	C	D
MQ29	A	B	C	<u>D</u>
MQ30	A	B	C	<u>D</u>

Answer Record Sheet: TEST 2

Reasoning

RQ1	<u>A</u>	B	C	D	E
RQ2	A	<u>B</u>	C	D	E
RQ3	A	B	C	<u>D</u>	E
RQ4	<u>A</u>	B	C	D	E
RQ5	A	B	C	D	<u>E</u>
RQ6	<u>A</u>	B	C	D	E
RQ7	A	B	<u>C</u>	D	E
RQ8	A	<u>B</u>	C	D	E
RQ9	A	B	C	<u>D</u>	E
RQ10	A	B	<u>C</u>	D	E
RQ11	A	B	C	D	<u>E</u>
RQ12	<u>A</u>	B	C	D	E
RQ13	A	B	C	D	<u>E</u>
RQ14	A	<u>B</u>	C	D	E
RQ15	<u>A</u>	B	C	D	E
RQ16	A	B	<u>C</u>	D	E
RQ17	A	B	C	<u>D</u>	E
RQ18	A	B	C	D	<u>E</u>
RQ19	A	<u>B</u>	C	D	E
RQ20	<u>A</u>	B	C	D	E
RQ21	A	B	C	D	<u>E</u>
RQ22	A	B	C	<u>D</u>	E
RQ23	A	<u>B</u>	C	D	E
RQ24	A	B	<u>C</u>	D	E
RQ25	A	<u>B</u>	C	D	E
RQ26	A	B	C	<u>D</u>	E
RQ27	A	B	C	D	<u>E</u>
RQ28	A	B	<u>C</u>	D	E
RQ29	A	<u>B</u>	C	D	E
RQ30	A	B	C	<u>D</u>	E

Verbal Ability

VQ1	A	B	C	D	<u>E</u>
VQ2	<u>A</u>	B	C	D	E
VQ3	A	B	<u>C</u>	D	E
VQ4	A	<u>B</u>	C	D	E
VQ5	A	B	C	D	<u>E</u>
VQ6	A	B	C	<u>D</u>	E
VQ7	A	B	<u>C</u>	D	E
VQ8	A	<u>B</u>	C	D	E
VQ9	A	B	C	<u>D</u>	E
VQ10	A	B	<u>C</u>	D	E
VQ11	A	<u>B</u>	C	D	E
VQ12	A	B	C	D	<u>E</u>
VQ13	A	B	<u>C</u>	D	E
VQ14	<u>A</u>	B	C	D	E
VQ15	A	<u>B</u>	C	D	E
VQ16	<u>A</u>	B	C	D	E
VQ17	A	<u>B</u>	C	D	E
VQ18	A	B	C	<u>D</u>	E
VQ19	<u>A</u>	B	C	D	E
VQ20	A	B	<u>C</u>	D	E
VQ21	A	B	C	<u>D</u>	E
VQ22	A	<u>B</u>	C	D	E
VQ23	<u>A</u>	B	C	D	E
VQ24	A	B	C	<u>D</u>	E
VQ25	<u>A</u>	B	C	D	E
VQ26	A	B	<u>C</u>	D	E
VQ27	A	<u>B</u>	C	D	E
VQ28	A	B	C	D	<u>E</u>
VQ29	A	B	C	<u>D</u>	E
VQ30	<u>A</u>	B	C	D	E

Answer Record Sheet: TEST 2

Numerical Reasoning

NQ1	<u>A</u>	B	C	D	E
NQ2	A	<u>B</u>	C	D	E
NQ3	A	B	<u>C</u>	D	E
NQ4	A	B	C	<u>D</u>	E
NQ5	A	B	C	D	<u>E</u>
NQ6	A	<u>B</u>	C	D	E
NQ7	A	B	C	D	<u>E</u>
NQ8	<u>A</u>	B	C	D	E
NQ9	A	B	<u>C</u>	D	E
NQ10	A	<u>B</u>	C	D	E
NQ11	A	B	C	<u>D</u>	E
NQ12	A	<u>B</u>	C	D	E
NQ13	A	B	<u>C</u>	D	E
NQ14	<u>A</u>	B	C	D	E
NQ15	A	B	C	<u>D</u>	E
NQ16	A	B	C	D	<u>E</u>
NQ17	A	B	<u>C</u>	D	E
NQ18	<u>A</u>	B	C	D	E
NQ19	A	B	C	<u>D</u>	E
NQ20	A	B	C	D	<u>E</u>
NQ21	A	<u>B</u>	C	D	E
NQ22	A	B	C	<u>D</u>	E
NQ23	<u>A</u>	B	C	D	E
NQ24	A	<u>B</u>	C	D	E
NQ25	A	B	<u>C</u>	D	E
NQ26	A	B	C	D	<u>E</u>
NQ27	A	B	C	<u>D</u>	E
NQ28	A	B	C	D	<u>E</u>
NQ29	<u>A</u>	B	C	D	E
NQ30	A	B	<u>C</u>	D	E

Mechanical Comprehension

MQ1	<u>A</u>	B	C	D
MQ2	A	<u>B</u>	C	D
MQ3	<u>A</u>	B	C	D
MQ4	A	B	C	<u>D</u>
MQ5	A	B	<u>C</u>	D
MQ6	A	B	<u>C</u>	D
MQ7	A	<u>B</u>	C	D
MQ8	A	B	<u>C</u>	D
MQ9	A	B	C	<u>D</u>
MQ10	<u>A</u>	B	C	D
MQ11	<u>A</u>	B	C	D
MQ12	A	<u>B</u>	C	D
MQ13	A	B	<u>C</u>	D
MQ14	A	B	C	<u>D</u>
MQ15	A	<u>B</u>	C	D
MQ16	A	B	C	<u>D</u>
MQ17	<u>A</u>	B	C	D
MQ18	A	B	<u>C</u>	D
MQ19	A	<u>B</u>	C	D
MQ20	A	B	C	<u>D</u>
MQ21	A	B	<u>C</u>	D
MQ22	<u>A</u>	B	C	D
MQ23	A	<u>B</u>	C	D
MQ24	A	B	C	<u>D</u>
MQ25	A	<u>B</u>	C	D
MQ26	A	B	C	<u>D</u>
MQ27	<u>A</u>	B	C	D
MQ28	A	B	<u>C</u>	D
MQ29	A	B	C	<u>D</u>
MQ30	<u>A</u>	B	C	D

Answer Record Sheet: TEST 3

Reasoning

RQ1	**A**	B	C	D	E
RQ2	A	B	C	**D**	E
RQ3	A	**B**	C	D	E
RQ4	A	B	C	D	**E**
RQ5	A	B	**C**	D	E
RQ6	**A**	B	C	D	E
RQ7	A	B	C	D	**E**
RQ8	A	**B**	C	D	E
RQ9	A	B	C	**D**	E
RQ10	A	B	C	D	**E**
RQ11	A	B	**C**	D	E
RQ12	A	**B**	C	D	E
RQ13	A	B	C	D	**E**
RQ14	A	B	C	**D**	E
RQ15	A	**B**	C	D	E
RQ16	A	B	C	**D**	E
RQ17	A	B	C	D	**E**
RQ18	**A**	B	C	D	E
RQ19	A	B	C	**D**	E
RQ20	A	B	**C**	D	E
RQ21	**A**	B	C	D	E
RQ22	A	**B**	C	D	E
RQ23	A	B	**C**	D	E
RQ24	A	B	C	D	**E**
RQ25	A	B	**C**	D	E
RQ26	A	B	C	**D**	E
RQ27	A	**B**	C	D	E
RQ28	A	B	C	D	**E**
RQ29	**A**	B	C	D	E
RQ30	A	B	**C**	D	E

Verbal Ability

VQ1	A	B	C	**D**	E
VQ2	A	**B**	C	D	E
VQ3	A	B	C	D	**E**
VQ4	A	B	C	**D**	E
VQ5	A	**B**	C	D	E
VQ6	A	B	**C**	D	E
VQ7	A	**B**	C	D	E
VQ8	A	B	C	**D**	E
VQ9	A	B	**C**	D	E
VQ10	A	B	C	D	**E**
VQ11	A	**B**	C	D	E
VQ12	**A**	B	C	D	E
VQ13	A	B	C	D	**E**
VQ14	A	B	**C**	D	E
VQ15	A	B	C	D	**E**
VQ16	A	B	C	**D**	E
VQ17	**A**	B	C	D	E
VQ18	A	**B**	C	D	E
VQ19	A	B	**C**	D	E
VQ20	A	B	C	**D**	E
VQ21	**A**	B	C	D	E
VQ22	A	B	**C**	D	E
VQ23	**A**	B	C	D	E
VQ24	A	B	C	**D**	E
VQ25	A	B	C	D	**E**
VQ26	A	B	C	**D**	E
VQ27	A	B	C	D	**E**
VQ28	A	**B**	C	D	E
VQ29	A	B	**C**	D	E
VQ30	A	B	C	D	**E**

Answer Record Sheet: TEST 3

Numerical Reasoning

NQ1	<u>A</u>	B	C	D	E
NQ2	A	<u>B</u>	C	D	E
NQ3	A	B	<u>C</u>	D	E
NQ4	A	B	C	<u>D</u>	E
NQ5	<u>A</u>	B	C	D	E
NQ6	A	<u>B</u>	C	D	E
NQ7	<u>A</u>	B	C	D	E
NQ8	A	B	C	D	<u>E</u>
NQ9	A	B	C	<u>D</u>	E
NQ10	A	B	C	D	<u>E</u>
NQ11	A	B	C	<u>D</u>	E
NQ12	A	<u>B</u>	C	D	E
NQ13	A	B	<u>C</u>	D	E
NQ14	A	<u>B</u>	C	D	E
NQ15	A	B	C	<u>D</u>	E
NQ16	A	B	<u>C</u>	D	E
NQ17	<u>A</u>	B	C	D	E
NQ18	A	B	<u>C</u>	D	E
NQ19	A	<u>B</u>	C	D	E
NQ20	A	B	C	D	<u>E</u>
NQ21	A	B	C	<u>D</u>	E
NQ22	A	B	C	D	<u>E</u>
NQ23	A	B	<u>C</u>	D	E
NQ24	<u>A</u>	B	C	D	E
NQ25	A	B	C	D	<u>E</u>
NQ26	A	B	C	<u>D</u>	E
NQ27	A	<u>B</u>	C	D	E
NQ28	A	B	<u>C</u>	D	E
NQ29	<u>A</u>	B	C	D	E
NQ30	A	B	C	D	<u>E</u>

Mechanical Comprehension

MQ1	A	<u>B</u>	C	D
MQ2	<u>A</u>	B	C	D
MQ3	A	B	C	<u>D</u>
MQ4	<u>A</u>	B	C	D
MQ5	A	B	<u>C</u>	D
MQ6	A	B	C	<u>D</u>
MQ7	A	B	C	<u>D</u>
MQ8	A	<u>B</u>	C	D
MQ9	A	<u>B</u>	C	D
MQ10	A	B	<u>C</u>	D
MQ11	A	<u>B</u>	C	D
MQ12	A	<u>B</u>	C	D
MQ13	<u>A</u>	B	C	D
MQ14	A	B	C	<u>D</u>
MQ15	A	B	<u>C</u>	D
MQ16	<u>A</u>	B	C	D
MQ17	<u>A</u>	B	C	D
MQ18	A	B	C	<u>D</u>
MQ19	A	B	<u>C</u>	D
MQ20	A	<u>B</u>	C	D
MQ21	<u>A</u>	B	C	D
MQ22	<u>A</u>	B	C	D
MQ23	A	B	C	<u>D</u>
MQ24	A	<u>B</u>	C	D
MQ25	A	B	<u>C</u>	D
MQ26	A	B	<u>C</u>	D
MQ27	A	B	C	<u>D</u>
MQ28	A	B	<u>C</u>	D
MQ29	<u>A</u>	B	C	D
MQ30	A	B	C	<u>D</u>

Answer Record Sheet: TEST 4

Reasoning

RQ1	<u>A</u>	B	C	D	E
RQ2	A	<u>B</u>	C	D	E
RQ3	A	B	<u>C</u>	D	E
RQ4	A	B	C	D	<u>E</u>
RQ5	<u>A</u>	B	C	D	E
RQ6	A	<u>B</u>	C	D	E
RQ7	A	B	<u>C</u>	D	E
RQ8	A	B	C	<u>D</u>	E
RQ9	A	<u>B</u>	C	D	E
RQ10	A	B	<u>C</u>	D	E
RQ11	A	B	C	D	<u>E</u>
RQ12	A	B	C	<u>D</u>	E
RQ13	<u>A</u>	B	C	D	E
RQ14	A	B	<u>C</u>	D	E
RQ15	A	B	C	D	<u>E</u>
RQ16	A	<u>B</u>	C	D	E
RQ17	A	B	C	<u>D</u>	E
RQ18	A	B	<u>C</u>	D	E
RQ19	A	B	C	<u>D</u>	E
RQ20	A	B	C	D	<u>E</u>
RQ21	A	<u>B</u>	C	D	E
RQ22	<u>A</u>	B	C	D	E
RQ23	A	B	C	D	<u>E</u>
RQ24	A	B	C	<u>D</u>	E
RQ25	<u>A</u>	B	C	D	E
RQ26	A	B	C	<u>D</u>	E
RQ27	A	B	<u>C</u>	D	E
RQ28	<u>A</u>	B	C	D	E
RQ29	A	B	C	<u>D</u>	E
RQ30	A	<u>B</u>	C	D	E

Verbal Ability

VQ1	<u>A</u>	B	C	D	E
VQ2	A	<u>B</u>	C	D	E
VQ3	A	B	C	D	<u>E</u>
VQ4	<u>A</u>	B	C	D	E
VQ5	A	B	C	D	<u>E</u>
VQ6	A	B	<u>C</u>	D	E
VQ7	A	B	C	<u>D</u>	E
VQ8	A	<u>B</u>	C	D	E
VQ9	<u>A</u>	B	C	D	E
VQ10	A	B	<u>C</u>	D	E
VQ11	A	B	C	<u>D</u>	E
VQ12	A	B	C	D	<u>E</u>
VQ13	A	<u>B</u>	C	D	E
VQ14	A	B	C	<u>D</u>	E
VQ15	A	B	<u>C</u>	D	E
VQ16	<u>A</u>	B	C	D	E
VQ17	A	B	C	<u>D</u>	E
VQ18	A	<u>B</u>	C	D	E
VQ19	A	B	<u>C</u>	D	E
VQ20	A	<u>B</u>	C	D	E
VQ21	A	B	C	<u>D</u>	E
VQ22	<u>A</u>	B	C	D	E
VQ23	A	B	C	<u>D</u>	E
VQ24	A	B	<u>C</u>	D	E
VQ25	A	<u>B</u>	C	D	E
VQ26	A	B	C	<u>D</u>	E
VQ27	<u>A</u>	B	C	D	E
VQ28	A	B	C	D	<u>E</u>
VQ29	A	B	<u>C</u>	D	E
VQ30	A	<u>B</u>	C	D	E

Answer Record Sheet: TEST 4

Numerical Reasoning

NQ1	A	B	C	D	<u>E</u>
NQ2	A	<u>B</u>	C	D	E
NQ3	<u>A</u>	B	C	D	E
NQ4	A	B	<u>C</u>	D	E
NQ5	A	B	<u>C</u>	D	E
NQ6	A	B	<u>C</u>	D	E
NQ7	A	<u>B</u>	C	D	E
NQ8	A	B	C	<u>D</u>	E
NQ9	A	B	C	D	<u>E</u>
NQ10	<u>A</u>	B	C	D	E
NQ11	A	B	C	<u>D</u>	E
NQ12	A	B	C	D	<u>E</u>
NQ13	A	<u>B</u>	C	D	E
NQ14	A	B	C	D	<u>E</u>
NQ15	A	B	<u>C</u>	D	E
NQ16	<u>A</u>	B	C	D	E
NQ17	A	<u>B</u>	C	D	E
NQ18	A	B	<u>C</u>	D	E
NQ19	A	B	C	<u>D</u>	E
NQ20	A	B	C	D	<u>E</u>
NQ21	A	B	<u>C</u>	D	E
NQ22	A	B	C	<u>D</u>	E
NQ23	A	B	C	D	<u>E</u>
NQ24	A	B	C	<u>D</u>	E
NQ25	<u>A</u>	B	C	D	E
NQ26	A	<u>B</u>	C	D	E
NQ27	A	B	C	<u>D</u>	E
NQ28	A	<u>B</u>	C	D	E
NQ29	A	B	C	D	<u>E</u>
NQ30	<u>A</u>	B	C	D	E

Mechanical Comprehension

MQ1	A	B	<u>C</u>	D
MQ2	<u>A</u>	B	C	D
MQ3	<u>A</u>	B	C	D
MQ4	A	<u>B</u>	C	D
MQ5	A	B	C	<u>D</u>
MQ6	A	<u>B</u>	C	D
MQ7	A	B	<u>C</u>	D
MQ8	A	B	C	<u>D</u>
MQ9	A	<u>B</u>	C	D
MQ10	A	<u>B</u>	C	D
MQ11	A	<u>B</u>	C	D
MQ12	A	B	<u>C</u>	D
MQ13	A	B	<u>C</u>	D
MQ14	A	B	<u>C</u>	D
MQ15	<u>A</u>	B	C	D
MQ16	<u>A</u>	B	C	D
MQ17	A	B	C	<u>D</u>
MQ18	A	B	C	<u>D</u>
MQ19	<u>A</u>	B	C	D
MQ20	<u>A</u>	B	C	D
MQ21	<u>A</u>	B	C	D
MQ22	A	B	<u>C</u>	D
MQ23	A	<u>B</u>	C	D
MQ24	A	B	C	<u>D</u>
MQ25	A	B	<u>C</u>	D
MQ26	<u>A</u>	B	C	D
MQ27	A	B	<u>C</u>	D
MQ28	A	B	C	<u>D</u>
MQ29	A	<u>B</u>	C	D
MQ30	A	<u>B</u>	C	D

EXPANDED ANSWERS: TEST 1

RQ1 C: 'Fraction' is the opposite of whole.

RQ2 D: 'Permanent' means the same as lasting.

RQ3 E: 'Gamble': you worship in a church and gamble in a casino.

RQ4 C: 6-sides is to 3-sides as 8-sides is to 4-sides.

RQ5 D: Take the smaller shape away from the left side of the larger.

RQ6 B: The shapes are split into equal parts: 2, 3, 4 then 5.

RQ7 D: We are adding 11 each time; 56 + 11 = 67

RQ8 A: Two methods: treat as two separate series: 28, 29, 30 then 31; or 28 plus 3, minus 2, plus 3, minus 2, plus 3, minus 2.

RQ9 D: 27 is three times 9 and 42 is three times 14.

RQ10 A: Easiest method: multiply the first pair of numbers by 4 so '50 to 20' is the same ratio as '200 to 80'.

RQ11 B: 'Devout' means the same as 'religious'.

RQ12 C: 'Like' means the opposite of 'loathe'.

RQ13 E: 'Street' is to 'road' as 'stream' is to 'river' (a larger version)

RQ14 D: This is the only shape without a straight line.

RQ15 E: Take the smaller shape from the left side of the larger shape.

RQ16 C: The entire shape rotates by 90^0 clockwise each time and the shading of the small interior shapes swaps over.

RQ17 A: Add 22 to get the next number: 78 + 22 = 100

RQ18 B: Add 4, then 5, then 6 and finally 7 to get 25.

RQ19 C: Multiply the first pair by 5 to give '100 is to 20'.

RQ20 E: Multiply the first pair by 3 to give '3 is to 13.5'.

RQ21 B: 'Disguise' means the same as 'conceal'.

RQ22 A: 'Dismissive' is the opposite of 'interested'.

RQ23 D: 'Gas is to solid' as 'steam is to ice'.

RQ24 C: Clockwise rotation of 180^0 or 90^0 twice.

RQ25 B: The shape becomes smaller but not too small.

RQ26 A: Intersecting lines: 1, 2, 3 then 4.

RQ27 D: Subtract 12, 11, 12, 11 then 49 − 12 = 37

RQ28 E: Add 16 each time; 49 + 16 = 65.

RQ29 B: Dividing 12.5 by 5 gives 2.5; then 150 ÷ 5 = 30.

RQ30 E: 18 is 12 x 1.5; then 8 x 1.5 = 12.

EXPANDED ANSWERS: TEST 1

VQ1 C: 'Off later' is two words not one word.

VQ2 D: 'Port wine' is two words not one word.

VQ3 E: There is no such word as innecessary.

VQ4 A: The other words are all types of sport.

VQ5 B: The other words are all types of fuel.

VQ6 E: The other words are all types of flower.

VQ7 C: 'Unfit to apply' means unsuitable, not physically unfit.

VQ8 E: 'Looking forward to' is being done in July makes no sense.

VQ9: D: 'Aspiration' meaning 'ambition' is the correct choice.

VQ10 A: 'Optimum' meaning 'best' is the correct choice.

VQ11 B: 'Rigid' is the opposite of the other choices.

VQ12 D: 'Naive' is the opposite of the other choices.

VQ13 C: 'Brick' does not belong with the other choices which are all forms of blocking.

VQ14 E: 'Veto' is similar to 'reject'.

VQ15 B: 'Unsure' is similar to 'doubtful'.

VQ16 C: 'Exempt' is similar to 'excused'.

VQ17 C: greenhouse and houseplant

VQ18 A: woodland and landfill

VQ19 C: boardwalk and walkabout

VQ20 B: shipowner and ownership

VQ21 D: new ideas and fresh ideas

VQ22 B: wheat and rice are both cereals

VQ23 A: paint colour and colour scheme

VQ24 E: The word 'state' is the best choice in this context.

VQ25 B: Only 'their' is grammatically correct.

VQ26 D: Only 'do' is grammatically correct.

VQ27 E: Only 'you're' meaning 'you are', is correct

VQ28 C: 'Hadn't' meaning 'had not been' is the correct choice.

VQ29 A: The word 'prosperous' is the best choice in this context.

VQ30 D: The word 'heavy' is the best choice because it fits with both the need for 'fitness' and the use of 'protective footwear'.

EXPANDED ANSWERS: TEST 1

NQ1 E: Add the two numbers longhand placing 426 below 3765.

NQ2 B: Recognise that 0.75 is three-quarters.

NQ3 A: 21639 to 3 s.f. is 216 followed by two noughts.

NQ4 C: 50 m wide (x2) plus 100 m long (x2) = 300 metres

NQ5 B: 22 x 45 = (20 x 45) +(2 x 45) = 900 + 90 = 990

NQ6 E: 80% x 120 = 8 times 10% of 120 = 8 x 12 = 96

NQ7 D: 24 – 20 + 14 = 4 + 14 = 18

NQ8 A: 1 x 1 divided by 2 x 3 = 1/6

NQ9 E: 15 minutes (quarter hour) then ¼ x 360^0 = 90^0

NQ10 A: 1.150$\underline{7}$7945 to 3 d.p. = 1.151 ('7 rounds to 10')

NQ11 C: 600 x 0.25 = 6 x 25 = 150

NQ12 C: 3522 – 489 = 3522 – 500 + 11 = 3022 + 11 = 3033

NQ13 D: 2/5 = 4/10 = 0.4

NQ14 B: 3.14159 (pi) to 3 s.f. = 3.14 (to 3 d.p. it is 3.142)

NQ15 C: 12 x 12 = 144; 4 sides x 12 = 48

NQ16 A: 575 ÷ 25; use multiplication: 20 x 25 = 500 and
3 x 25 = 75. 20 + 3 = 23. (23 x 25 = 575)

NQ17 D: 10% of £111 = £111.00 ÷ 10 = £11.10;
then £111.00 - £11.10 = £99.90

NQ18 B: x = 29 and y is 3x, so y = 29 x 3 = 87; then y – x becomes
87 – 29 = 58. Alternatively: y = 3x; so y – x = 3x – x = 2x = 58

NQ19 A: Add the whole numbers and fractions separately: 2 + 4 = 6; ½
+ ¾ = ½ + ½ + ¼ = 1¼; finally 6 +1¼ = 7¼

NQ20: D: 40 minutes is 40/60 hours = 4/6 or 2/3 hours;
finally one-third of 360^0 is 120^0 so two-thirds is 240^0.

NQ21 E: 0.00567 to 2 s.f. is 0.0057 (the 6 is increased to a 7).

NQ22 B: 4000 x 0.001 = 4 x 1.0 = 4

NQ23 D: 4:1 = 4 parts sand and 1 part cement; total parts
= 4 + 1 = 5; one cubic metre is 1/5 cement = 0.2

NQ24 C: two thirds = 0.666 = 0.667 to 3 d.p. because the fourth
decimal place is also a 6 (0.666$\underline{6}$ rounds up to 0.667)

NQ25 E: 1/8 x 100% = 100 ÷ 8 = 12.5; then 3/8 = 37.5

NQ26 A: 1/2 ÷ 3/8 = 1/2 x 8/3 = 1x8/2x3 = 8/6 = $1^{2/6}$ =$1^{1/3}$

NQ27 A: 6 divides into 12 twice and 18 three times

NQ28 C: 96 km x 5/8; division first 96 ÷ 8 = 12; then 12 x 5 = 60

NQ29 B: 2.5 x 360 = 2 x 360 + 0.5 x 360 = 720 + 180 = 900.

NQ30 D: 8 ÷ 24 = 1/3; then 1/3 x 360 = 120.

EXPANDED ANSWERS: TEST 1

MQ1 B: Similar polls repel (and opposite poles attract).

MQ2 C: Larger at the base with more of its weight nearer the ground.

MQ3 A: 7 – 1 = 6 moving ropes (last rope pulls downs); 420 ÷ 6 = 70

MQ4 C: All 3 bulbs are in parallel, so each receive the full voltage. Circuit B has the second brightest bulbs and circuit A the least bright.

MQ5 B: The beam can only balance at a point between the weights.

MQ6: D: All the same; the water pressure depends only on the depth.

MQ7 C: Only valve 5 must to be closed (2, 3 and 4 can be left open).

MQ8 A: Enters at A, piston moves left; enters at B, piston moves right.

MQ9 D: The pressure is hydrostatic (weight of the liquid above).

MQ10 C: The container with the smallest base fills to the line first (the other vessels then catch up, filling to the top in the same time).

MQ11 A: shortening out a bulb (i.e. with a wire); A and D reduce the current and C breaks the circuit.

MQ12 B: water is heavier than oil; more water equals more pressure.

MQ13 C: '3' rotates clockwise, '2' anti-clockwise and '1' clockwise.

MQ14 B: Both balls take two seconds to hit the ground so the second ball must be travelling at 100 metres per second.

MQ15 D: In any system of gears the first and last gears rotate at the same speed if they have the same number of teeth.

MQ16 A: There are 5 supporting ropes: 10 kg ÷ 5 = 2 kg per rope.

MQ17 D: Bulbs A, B and D illuminate; C has no positive supply.

MQ18 B: The symbol for a capacitor (two parallel plates).

MQ19 C: When bulb 1 is removed bulb 2 has no positive supply.

MQ20 C: As the head of water drops, the water empties more slowly.

MQ21 A: No bulbs illuminate because there is no negative return.

MQ22 B: The two vertical switches only. Four bulbs will illuminate if the horizontal switch at the top is closed, even with the others open.

MQ23 A: The symbol for a diode; current flows in the direction shown by the triangle.

MQ24 D: C has the most kinetic energy but no potential energy; A has the most potential energy but no kinetic energy; B' has half of each.

MQ25 A: Three springs stretch 4 cm each as does the single spring.

MQ26 B: Both rotate anticlockwise; wheel 3 is the easiest to envisage.

MQ27 C: Gears 1 and 3 must rotate ACW, so 2 is CW and 4 is ACW.

MQ28 B: Colder air heavier; the balloon displaces more weight of air.

MQ29 D: Left: 50x1=50. Right: 10x4 + 1xX; so 50 = 40 + X; X =10

MQ30 D: X = 20 rpm; pair on same shaft = 10 rpm; then Y = 5 rpm.

EXPANDED ANSWERS: TEST 2

RQ1 A: 'Authentic' means the same as 'real'.

RQ2 B: 'Uniform' is the opposite of 'different'.

RQ3 D: 'Circle is to square' (2-d) as 'sphere is to cube' (3-d).

RQ4 A: Larger triangle, unshaded containing larger square shaded (and shading slants is in the opposite direction).

RQ5 E: Only the last pair are not mirror images/reflections.

RQ6 A: Two rules: 1. larger shape has a shaded smaller copy; and 2. shaded shape rotates through 90^0.

RQ7 C: 35,45 then 55 and 203,193 then 183.

RQ8 B: Rule: $3^2,4^2,5^2,6^2,7^2$ then $8^2 = 64$; or $+7,+9,+11,+13,+15 = 64$

RQ9 D: A half is two-quarters and a third is two-sixths.

RQ10 C: Multiply by 10 to get from the first number to the second number (decimal point moves one place to the right).

RQ11 E: 'Robust' means the same as 'resilient'.

RQ12 A: 'Restrict' is the opposite of 'free'.

RQ13 E: A 'book' is found in a 'library' and a 'painting' in a 'gallery'.

RQ14 B: Rule: rotate 45^0 clockwise.

RQ15 A: Take the small triangle away from the left side of the large.

RQ16 C: Rule: the number of overlapping shaded areas increase by one from left to right: none, one, two, so the next is three.

RQ17 D: Two series: 12, 24, 36, then 48 (also 20, 19, 18, then 17).

RQ18 E: Rule: add 5, 10, 15, 20, 25 to give 80, then 30 to give 110.

RQ19 B: Rule 60 is 1.5 times 40 and 45 is 1.5 times 30.

RQ20 A: 12 is 60 times larger than 1/5 (five fifths are one whole and we have 12 wholes), then 1/6 x 60 times larger = 10.

RQ21: E: 'Accomplish' means the same as 'achieve'.

RQ22: D: 'Detriment' is the opposite of 'advantage'.

RQ23 B: Rule: tyre is made of rubber; wheel is made of alloy.

RQ24 C: Turn the shape upside down; add it to itself.

RQ25 B: Subtract the smaller shape to leave the small diamond.

RQ26 D: All the other shapes have 5 sides (not 6)

RQ27 E: Rule: +3, +4, +5, +6, then +7 = 41 and +8 = 49

RQ28 C: Rule: +0.5, +1.0, +1.5, +2.0, then +2.5 = 10.2

RQ29 B: Multiply the first two numbers by 30 to give 120 is to 90:

RQ30 D: Multiply the first pair by 2.5 to give 0.25 is to 15

EXPANDED ANSWERS: TEST 2

VQ1 E: There is no such word as 'homebargain' (home bargain).

VQ2 A: There is no such word as 'noway' (no way).

VQ3 C: There is no such word as 'overdifficult' (over difficult).

VQ4 B: These are all 'dwellings'.

VQ5 E: 'Hygienic' is the best choice because it includes something from all four of the remaining answer choices.

VQ6 D: These are all types of 'gas'.

VQ7 C: This is one choice of menu unlike the others which have two.

VQ8 B: This says the hitting was done by the back of the red car which is not the same as into the back of the blue car.

VQ9 D: This suggests that the early start will be the following day.

VQ10 C: This sentence refers to Mike's class and not Mike himself.

VQ11 B: 'Associated' is the correct choice; not that only 'associated' and 'found' can be placed in front of 'with'.

VQ12 E: 'Liaison' is the best choice in the context of the sentence, because it means co-operation and communication.

VQ13 C: 'Frail' is the opposite of the other four words.

VQ14 A: 'Sand' is the odd one out; the others are forms of transport.

VQ15 B: 'Teacher' is the odd word out; the others are all 'learners'.

VQ16 A: 'Punctual' is similar to 'early'; the rest are linked to lateness.

VQ17 B: 'Relevant' is similar to 'suited'; it is the most comparable.

VQ18 D: 'Clear' is similar to 'transparent'; the others are opposites.

VQ19 A: 'Houseboat' and 'boatload'.

VQ20 C: 'Runway' and 'wayward'.

VQ21 D: 'Keypad' and 'padlock'.

VQ22 B: 'Outback' and 'backdated'.

VQ23 A: 'Ship' as in 'ferry' and 'ship' as in 'deliver'.

VQ24 D: 'Change' as in 'shape' and 'change' as in 'transform'

VQ25 A: 'Worry' as in 'upset' and 'worry' as in 'alarm'.

VQ26 C: 'They've' meaning 'they have'.

VQ27 B: 'Those' new venues were (plural past tense). Compare this with: 'These new venues are' (plural present tense). 'This new venue is' (singular present tense). 'This new venue was' (singular past).

VQ28 E: 'The team is' (present singular tense); used in preference to 'the team are' because team is used as a collective noun.

VQ29 D: 'Flippant' means not serious.

VQ30 A: 'Scrutinizing' meaning examining carefully in detail.

EXPANDED ANSWERS: TEST 2

NQ1 A: Subtract the two numbers placing the 275 below the 3172.

NQ2 B: 45% means 45/100; cancel top/bottom by 5 to give 9/20.

NQ3 C: The fourth s.f. in 1407 is 7, which is greater than 5, so the 7 is rounded up to 10, so that 1407 to 3 s.f. is 1410.

NQ4 D: Half base x height (multiply the two numbers and divide by 2).

NQ5 E: Mental arithmetic: 30x120 = 3600; 2x120 = 240, total 3840.

NQ6 B: 80 x 65% = 52; method: 10% of 80 = 8, so 60% = 6x8 = 48; if 10% = 8 then 5% = 4; finally 48 + 4 = 52.

NQ7 E: Mental arithmetic: 75 – 215; recognise that adding back 140 to 75 = 215 or subtract 75 from both numbers to give 0 – 140 = -140

NQ8: A: turn the right-hand side upside down and multiply: 5/6 ÷ 5/8 becomes 5/6 x 8/5, now cancel the 5's to leave 8/6 or 1 whole + 2/6

NQ9: C: Set up the fraction as 50/60; then calculate 50/60 x 360; or 5/6 x 360; one-sixth of 360 is 60 so five-sixths are 300.

NQ10 B: 1.15077945 to 3 s.f. The first 3 digits are 1.15 (and the fourth digit is zero, which rounds down to zero) hence we have 1.15

NQ11 D: Move dp to the larger number: 250 x 0.04 = 2.5 x 4 = 10.

NQ12 B: 30 x 15 x 10 = 450 x 10 = 4500 cm^3; then ÷ 1000 = 4.5 L

NQ13 C: Method 19/25 = 76/100 (x4 top/bottom); 76.0 ÷ 100= 0.76

NQ14 A: 3.14159 to 4 d.p. = 3.1415 with the 5 increased to 6: 3.1416

NQ15 D: Method: 44 divided into 4 equal sides = 11; 11 x 11 = 121

NQ16 E: 1040 ÷ 20 = 104 ÷ 2 = 54

NQ17 C: Method: approximate £8.95 to £9; calculate how many can be bought for £100; double it. £100 ÷ 9 = 11 (£1 left); 11 x 2 = 22

NQ18 A: s x t – s = 9 x 16 – 9 = 90+54 – 9 = 144 – 9 = 135; or recognize that 9 x 16 – 9 = 'fifteen nines' (15 x 9 = 135).

NQ19 D: 3¾ x 8 = 3x8 + ¾ x 8 = 24 + 6 = 30; (¾x8 = ½x8 + ¼x8)

NQ20 E: 45/60 = ¾; ¾ x 360 = 270 (½x360 = 180; ¼x360 = 90).

NQ21 B: 21.04568 to 3 s.f. is 21.0 or 21 (fourth digit rounds to 0).

NQ22 D: 10000 x 0.125 = 10 x 125 = 1250

NQ23 A: 45:5; 9+1= 10 parts; 1 part = 50÷10 = 5; then 9 parts = 45

NQ24 B: 1/9 or 1÷9 = 0.1111 etc, so 5/9 = 0.5555 etc; 2 d.p. = 0.56

NQ25 C: Full rectangle = 5x10 = 50; shaded = ¼; ¼ x 50 = 12.5

NQ26 E: 6 ÷ 3/7 = 6 x 7/3 = 6 x 7 ÷ 3 = 6 ÷ 3 x 7 = 2 x 7 = 14

NQ27 D: Multiples of 6: 6,12,18,24,30 etc and of 8: 8,16,24,32,40 etc

NQ28 E: 1.6 x 25; 1.6 x 10 = 16; 1.6 x 5 = 8; then 16 + 16 + 8 = 40

NQ29 A: 3 x 360 = 3 x 300 + 3 x 60 = 900 + 180 = 1080

NQ30 C: fraction is 1/12 (1 hour out of 12 hours); 1/12 x 360 = 20

EXPANDED ANSWERS: TEST 2

MQ1 A: The weight is distributed over the largest area on the ground.

MQ2 B: Balls bounce off each other to revere their direction of travel.

MQ3 A: The far left coupling carries the weight of all three (1750 kg).

MQ4 D: This is the only bulb is in a circuit by itself (sees full voltage).

MQ5 C: Shallowest gradient offers the greatest mechanical advantage.

MQ6 C: You have to place the 10 kg weight twice as distant from the fulcrum as the 20 kg weight in order to balance it

MQ7 B: 12 teeth to 6 = x2; 6 teeth to 3 = x2; then 2 x 2 x 120 = 480.

MQ8 D: A = 100 ÷ 2 = 50; B = 100 ÷ 2 = 50; C = 150 ÷ 3 = 50.

MQ9 D: All the bulbs have a positive and negative supply.

MQ10 A: Not the adjacent wheels (6, 4); 3 will, not 2, 1 will (1,3,5).

MQ11 A: Climbs up: MA = 20m ÷ 10m = 2; balance weight for a 50 kg trolley is 50 ÷ 2 = 25 kg and we have 30 kg with no friction.

MQ12 B: The greatest depth below the surface of the water.

MQ13 C: 50 (not 500) because the area of a piston is proportional to its diameter squared (10:1 diameters = 100:1 areas).

MQ14: D: FSD = 240 V. The scale split into 4 equal intervals of 60 V each with graduation marks at (reading from left to right) 0, 60, 120, 180 and 240. The arrow is mid-way between 180 and 240 (i.e. 210).

MQ15 B: The symbol for an earth connection (usually the negative).

MQ16 D: Wide base with a narrower top (lowest centre of gravity).

MQ17 A: The top three gear must all rotate clockwise (CW) but the gear beneath the chain rotates ACW and slower than the smaller gear.

MQ18 C: MA = 4, so 4 metres of rope are pulled for 1 metre of drag.

MQ19 B: pos-pos-pos; neg-neg-neg; batteries wired in parallel = 12 V.

MQ20 D: Two batteries connected in series (neg to pos); 6+6 = 12 V; however the connections on the meter are reversed so its -12V.

MQ21 C: Lowest/most submerged surface has the greatest pressure.

MQ22 A: Weight A looks smaller than B but must it must be heavier than B and C combined since it is nearer to the fulcrum .

MQ23 B: P3 only. P1 will fall and P2 will easily tip over.

MQ24 D: Same as W. Consider only the first and last in any system.

MQ25 B: The air travels a greater distance in the same time.

MQ26 D: B is ½ stiff as A with ½ weight; C is x2 stiff but x2 weight.

MQ27 A: The Skydiver is falling due to the force of gravity.

MQ28 C: The pressure is the lowest where the speed is the highest.

MQ29 D: Maximum potential energy achieved at the maximum height.

MQ30 A: Cancel the 100 g's; mark scale 1,2,3,4,5 then: Left (40x1) + 'X' x3. Right (10x1) + (30x3). So 40 + 3X= 100; 3X = 60, X = 20

EXPANDED ANSWERS: TEST 3

RQ1 A: 'Ascertain' means the same as 'determine'.

RQ2 D: 'Compress' is the opposite of 'stretch'.

RQ3 B: A car carries passengers and a ship carries cargo.

RQ4 E: The 3-d shape when viewed from the top.

RQ5 C: The only non-triangular shaped shading.

RQ6 A: Rotation is 90 degrees anticlockwise each time.

RQ7 E: Two series together: 25, 50, 75, 100, and 30, 60, 90, 120.

RQ8 B: +5, +10, +20, +40; so the next is +80; (81 + 80 = 161)

RQ9 D: 75 is to 5 as 60 is to 4 because 75 is 15 x 5 and 60 is 15 x 4.

RQ10 E: 30 is to 100 as 24 is to 80: 100 is three and one-third times 30; then 24 times three and one-third is 72 + 8 = 80

RQ11 C: 'Dismiss' means the same as 'reject'.

RQ12 B: 'Strict' is the opposite of 'lenient'.

RQ13 E: Electricity flows along a cable and water flows along a pipe.

RQ14 D: The number of sides: A = 8, B = 8, C = 8, D = 12, E = 8

RQ15 B: Take the smaller shape from the base of the larger shape.

RQ16 D: 1st step: arrows reverse so eliminate B,C and E (leaves A and D); 2nd step: triangle rotates 90^0 clockwise as per D.

RQ17 E: minus 12, minus 11, minus 10, then minus 9 (39 – 9 = 30).

RQ18 A: These are all prime numbers; the next primes are 17 and 19.

RQ19 D: 64 is 8 x 8 (8 squared) and 25 is 5 x 5 (5 squared).

RQ20 C: Multiplying the first pair of numbers '0.1 is to 2.25' by 100 gives: '10 is to 225'.

RQ21 A: 'Inclination' means the same as 'tendency'.

RQ22 B: 'Obstruct is the opposite of 'encourage'.

RQ23 C: Cement is a constituent of concrete; O_2 is a component of air.

RQ24 E: Reflection (not rotation); only E has the both the line and the shapes in the correct position, with the shapes the correct way up.

RQ25 C: The top line moves down and the bottom line move up with the balls on opposite ends.

RQ26 D: Eliminate A (wrong way up), B and E (two shaded shapes) and C (same as the last shape); leaves only D (120^0 ACW rotation).

RQ27 B: Two series together: 2, 4, 6, 8, (10) and 16, 13, 10, then 7.

RQ28 E: One series: +5, +6, +7, then + 8 = 27, with + 9 = 36.

RQ29 A: Multiplying the first pair of numbers '0.5 is to 6' by 24 gives '12 is to 144'. Alternatively: 6 is twelve times 0.5; twelve x 12 = 144.

RQ30 C: Multiplying the first pair '1/8 is to 2' by 8 gives '1 is to 16'.

EXPANDED ANSWERS: TEST 3

VQ1 D: There is now such word as 'outnow' (out now).
VQ2 B: There is no such word as 'stopshort' (stop short)
VQ3 E: There is no such word as 'showup' (show up)
VQ4 D: These are all types of 'vehicle'.
VQ5 B: These are all forms of 'book'.
VQ6 C: These are all forms of 'shoe'.
VQ7 B: The weather is referred to in the 'past tense' not the future.
VQ8 D: This is the only sentence to say that the car stopped.
VQ9 C: The application is put before the fitness test in this sentence.
VQ10 A: This in the only sentence to say that the negative is first.
VQ11 B: 'Fork' because the other items are used for cutting.
VQ12 A: 'Apple' because the other fruits have a stone in the middle.
VQ13 E: 'Manchester' is not a capital city.
VQ14 C: 'Agree' and 'concur' are similar in meaning.
VQ15 E: 'Valid' means 'true'.
VQ16 D: 'Clumsy' and 'unwieldy' are similar in meaning.
VQ17 A: 'waterwheel' and 'wheelhouse'
VQ18 B: 'paperback' and 'backspace'
VQ19 C: 'thumbwheel' and 'wheelchair'
VQ20 D: 'headmaster' and 'mastermind'
VQ21 A: 'Honest fits with both 'straight' and 'true'.
VQ22 C: 'Abandon' fits both 'desert' and 'leave'
VQ23 A: 'Mirror' fits both 'parrot' and 'echo'.
VQ24 D: 'all ready to' is the correct grammar; all the class were ready.
VQ25 E: 'should've' meaning should have; 'of' never replaces 'have'.
VQ26 D: 'dependent' (not 'dependant' as in a child or spouse).
VQ27 E: 'There's meaning 'there is' (not 'theirs' as in belonging to).
VQ28 B: 'Least' (or most) is used when comparing three.
VQ29 C: 'Value' is the best choice in the context of the sentence.
VQ30 E: 'Relevant' is the best choice in the context of the sentence.

EXPANDED ANSWERS: TEST 3

NQ1 A: Subtract 100 and add 11; then 298 − 89 = 198 + 11 = 209.

NQ2 B: 85p/100p = 85/100 = 17/20 by dividing the top/bottom by 5.

NQ3 C: 24859.82 to two s.f. is 25 followed by three noughts (25000).

NQ4 D: 2 x 2 x 2 cm; each face = 4 cm^2; x 6 faces = 24 cm^2.

NQ5 A: Mental arithmetic: 33 x 11 = 33 x 10 + 33 = 330 + 33 = 363

NQ6 B: 55% = 55 out of 100 which is the same as 110 out of 200.

NQ7 A: Convert to twelfths: 3/4 − 2/3 = 9/12 − 8/12 = 1/12

NQ8 E: 2/3 ÷ ¼ = 2/3 x 4/1 = 8/3 = 2 wholes (6/3) + 2/6 or 2 1/3

NQ9 D: 1 hour = 1/12 of 360^0 = 30^0 so 5 hours = 5 x 30 = 150^0.

NQ10 E: 1.15077945 to 2 s.f. = 1.2 (round up 0.15 to 0.2).

NQ11 D: 1750 x 0.002 = 1.75 x 2 = 3.5 (move dp to larger number).

NQ12 B: 2.26 (compare units then tenths then hundredths).

NQ13 C: To express 3/8 as a decimal divide 8 into 3.000 longhand or use well known fractions and decimals, starting with one-eighth:
1/8 is half of 1/4, or half of 0.25 which is 0.125; then x3 = 0.375

NQ14 B: 3.14159 to 3 d.p. is 3.142 (0.1415 rounds to 0.142)

NQ15 D: 900 cm^2 = 30 cm x 30 cm; 4 sides x 30 cm = 120 cm.

NQ16 C: 625 ÷ 25; multiply both numbers by 4; so 2500 ÷ 100 = 25

NQ17 A: 5 hours = 5 x 60 = 300 minutes; use trial and improvement:
ten 35's = 350; nine 35's = 315; eight 35's = 280 (eight lessons max)

NQ18 C: $v(v − u)$ = 10(10 − 7.5) = 10x(2.5) = 25.

NQ19 B: 1¼ x 90 = 1x90 + ¼x90 = 90 + 90/4 (or 45/2) = 90 + 22.5 = 112.5.   Alternative: 'remove' the fraction by multiplying the mixed fraction by 4 whilst dividing the 90 by 4 to balance:1¼ x 90 = 5 x 22.5

NQ20 E: Full circle = 12 hrs; 8/12 = 2/3; 360^0 x 2/3 = 120 x 2 = 240^0

NQ21 D: 0.04896 to 3 s.f. is: 0.049 (the 8 rounds up to a 9).

NQ22 E: 14499 to the nearest ten is 14500 (99 rounds to 100)

NQ23 C: Multiply 14.5 x 8. Use longhand or place values as in 14.5 = 10 + 4 + ½; multiplying each of these by 8 gives 80 + 32 + 4 = 116

NQ24 A: 75.54 % means 75.54/100, which is 0.7554; to 1d.p = 0.8

NQ25 E: The crossed lines are there two show that the shape consists of two identical squares each of side 12 cm; 6 sides x 12 cm = 72 cm.

NQ26 D: Factors of 8: 1, 2, <u>4</u>, 8; factors of 12; 1, 2, 3, <u>4</u>, 6,12

NQ27 B: 5½ ÷ 3 = 11÷ 6 (double both) = 1 whole (6 sixths) + 5/6.

NQ28 C: 0.621371192 x 1<u>0000</u> = 6213.71192 (by moving the dp <u>4</u> places to the right) which gives 6214 to the nearest whole mile.

NQ29 A: 6 revs = 6 x 360^0 = 6 x 300 + 6 x 60 = 1800 + 360 = 2160^0

NQ30 E: 1 hour = 12th rotation (like 5 mins); 1/12 x 360^0 = 30^0 so half an hour = 15^0

EXPANDED ANSWERS: TEST 3

MQ1 B: The circle and the triangle will fit inside the square.

MQ2 A: MA = 5; 100 cm ÷ 5 = 20 cm

MQ3 D: I is current measured in Amps.

MQ4 A: The largest gear rotates the slowest in any connected system.

MQ5 C: This symbol is used for a light emitting diode (LED); note that without the two arrows it would be an ordinary diode.

MQ6 D: The horizontal speed increases in the order A, B then C; however, the vertical speed of all three balls is the same.

MQ7 D: All three objects are static, though only the spoon is stable.

MQ8 B: Less than 1 (front driven gear larger than rear output gear).

MQ9 B: Wide handle = more torque (long handle = more leverage).

MQ10 C: The two bulbs on the right (the left has no negative supply).

MQ11 B: The short shelves B and C create the least leverage; B has its deepest screw where the leverage is highest (lever = force x distance).

MQ12 B: The weight is nearest to the fulcrum; greatest MA.

MQ13 A: The smaller the centre shaft the greater the MA.

MQ14 D: 68 ^{0}C. Four graduations along from 60; each interval = 2 ^{0}C.

MQ15 C: Both (top three are in series; bottom pair are in parallel).

MQ16 A: 'T' (pull) is highest where the pendulum moves the quickest.

MQ17 A: Place the load over the wheel for the best MA (leverage).

MQ18 D: The inner wheels turn ACW when the outer wheels turn CW.

MQ19 C: The balance reads 3 kg; the force is 1.5 kg since the MA = 2.

MQ20 B: The most dense block will float the lowest (though it is not necessarily the heaviest). Block sinks if more dense than liquid.

MQ21 A: 5 amps (same power out; V x A = 120 Watt both sides)

MQ22 A: 45^0 is the correct angle (90^0 split in half).

MQ23 D: Stretch = 5 cm per kg; extra 4 kg = 5 kg in total; the new stretch is given by 5 x 5 cm = 25 cm

MQ24 B: The pair of bulbs in the centre are the dimmest because there are three bulbs in the loop that the current must take (not two).

MQ25 C: The longest pendulum swings the slowest (longest 'period') whatever the weight on the end.

MQ26 C: The load is more difficult to lift (MA less than 1; no multiplier)

MQ27 D: 1 rev 12 teeth gear = 11/3 revs 9 teeth gear; i.e. +200 rpm.

MQ28 C: 3 Tonne at C = 6 Tonne at B = 12 Tonne at A. (Force x dist).

MQ29 A: The poles have been shorted out in B2 and B3; (B2 negative to positive; B3 positive to negative on bulb; B1 negative to negative).

MQ30 D: Force x dist: A = 30; B = 45 ÷ 1.5 = 30; C = 15 ÷ 0.5 = 30.

EXPANDED ANSWERS: TEST 4

RQ1 A: 'Opportune' means the same as 'fortunate'

RQ2 B: 'Limited' is the opposite of 'infinite'.

RQ3 C: 'Sugar' is the building block of carbohydrate as 'amino acid' is the building block of protein.

RQ4 E: Shapes total 8 lines; A, B, C and D total 7 lines.

RQ5 A: Rotation is 90^0 clockwise.

RQ6 B: 7 small blocks continue the sequence 10, 9, 8...

RQ7 C: Minus 11, 10, 9, 8 and finally 7 (61 – 7 = 54).

RQ8 D: Half, third, half, third and finally half (½ x 16 = 8).

RQ9 B: Multiply the pair '10 is to 2' by 1.5 to give '15 is to 3'.

RQ10 C: Multiplying 1.5 by 20 gives 30; multiplying 1/8 x 20 gives 20/8 = 2 wholes and 4/8 = 2.5

RQ11 E: 'Infallible' means the same as 'foolproof'.

RQ12 D: 'Precedent' is the opposite of 'later' (and same as A,B,C,E).

RQ13 A: Exaggerate 'accident' to get 'catastrophe'; exaggerate luck to get 'windfall'.

RQ14 C: Rotation is 90^0 clockwise.

RQ15 E: Small shaded shape has a larger unshaded pair (except E).

RQ16 B: Compare the first two boxes: larger triangle inverts; small central shape has a shaded pair; stripes slope in the opposite direction. Apply these rules to the third box.

RQ17 D: Add 6, 12, 24 (doubling), next is add 48 (47 + 48 = 95).

RQ18 C: Two series together: 1,2,3,4,5 and 9,8,7,6 so the next is 5.

RQ19 D: Divide the first pair by 4 to give '8 is to 2' as '2 is to ½.

RQ20 E: Multiply the first pair by 3 to give '$2x$ is to $5y$' as '$6x$ is $15y$'.

RQ21 B: 'Disarray' means the same as 'chaos'.

RQ22 A: 'Omit' is the opposite 'include'.

RQ23 E: Money can lead to prosperity (money improved) in the same way as a job can lead to a career (job improved).

RQ24 D: Only D has all the blocks and spaces in the same positions.

RQ25 A: Rules: the small shapes rotate one position clockwise (only A and B do this) and the central shape remains unchanged (so not B).

RQ26 D: Rule: The P, W, M, and Z with a vertical line, are drawn with four straight lines.

RQ27 C: Rules: x1, x2, x3, x4 (= 24) then x 5 = 120.

RQ28 A: Two series: 32,30,28 then 26 (also 29,27,25,23); alternative method: minus 3, plus 1, minus 3, plus 1, minus 3, then 25 + 1 = 26.

RQ29 D: Multiply the first pair by 8 to give '9 is to 8' as '72 is to 64'.

RQ30 B: Multiply the first pair by 16 to give '4 is to 1' as '64 is to 16'.

EXPANDED ANSWERS: TEST 4

VQ1 A: There is no such word as 'tenmen' (ten men).

VQ2 B: There is no such word as 'pinnumber' (pin number).

VQ3 E: There is no such word as 'handchosen' (hand chosen).

VQ4 A: These are all boats.

VQ5 E: These are all forms of precipitation.

VQ6 C: These are all drinks.

VQ7 D: Here 'only' is linked with 'I' instead of with the weekend.

VQ8 B: This sentence compares the understanding of the two people rather than stating that neither person understands.

VQ9 A: This sentence states the exact opposite of the others.

VQ10 C: 'Missing' is linked with 'details' instead of with 'message'.

VQ11 D: 'An informed decision' (links with 'sufficient information').

VQ12 E: 'Skill deficiencies' (links with the opposite of 'strengths')

VQ13 B: 'Size' is not one of the five senses.

VQ14 D: A 'bed' is not a seat.

VQ15 C: A 'ruler' is not for writing or drawing.

VQ16 A: 'Inept' is similar to 'clumsy'.

VQ17 D: 'Precursor' is similar to 'precede' (comes before).

VQ18 B: 'Protocol' is similar to 'rules'.

VQ19 C: 'Roadworks' and 'workshops'.

VQ20 B: 'Doorstop' and 'stopgap'.

VQ21 D: 'Playground' and 'groundsheet'.

VQ22 A: 'Birdsong' and 'songbird'.

VQ23 D: 'cutlery' items.

VQ24 C: 'retain' means store and keep.

VQ25 B: 'extent' means degree and area.

VQ26 D: 'likelihood' meaning chance, is the best choice in this context.

VQ27 A: 'interesting' artefacts is the best choice in a police context.

VQ28 E: 'encourage' is the best choice in the context of the sentence.

VQ29 C: 'detrimental' (harmful) links with poor performance.

VQ30 B: 'disrupt' links with a change to a normal daily routine.

EXPANDED ANSWERS: TEST 4

NQ1 E: 80x250 = 8x2500 = 8x2000 + 8x500 = 16000+4000 =20000.

NQ2 B: 25 to 30 = +5; 5/25 = 1/5 = 20% (20/100).

NQ3 A: 243610 to 3 s.f. = 244 and three zeros. i.e. 244000.

NQ4 C: Breadth = 100/4 = 25; Perimeter = 100+25+100+25 = 250.

NQ5 C: 32x120 = 32x100 + 32x20 (or 32x10x2) = 3200+640 = 3840.

NQ6 C: 64/80; increase 80 by ¼ to give 100; increase 64 by ¼ to match; so we have 64/80 = (64+16)/(80 + 20) = 80/100 = 80%

NQ7 B: $y - 2x$ = 95 – 2 x 18 = 95 – 36 = 59.

NQ8 D: 2¾ + 1½ = 2¾ + (¼ + 1¼) = 3 + 1¼ = 4¼

NQ9 E: 55/60 x 360 = 55 ÷ 60 x 360 = 55 x 360 ÷ 60 = 55 x 6 = 330

NQ10 A: 384400 to the nearest 1000 is 384000 (the 4400 is rounded down to 4000 rather than up to 5000).

NQ11 D: 4440 x 0.002 = 4.44 x 2 = 8.88 (d.p. moved to larger no.)

NQ12 E: 50 liters = 50 x 1000 ml = 50000 ml (same as 50000 cm^3); base area = 40cm x 50cm = 2000 cm^2; finally depth = 50000 ÷ 2000 = 50 ÷ 2 = 25 cm deep.

NQ13 B: 32/40 = 8/10 (cancel top and bottom by 4 (or by 2 twice); then 8/10 = 80/100 = 80%.

NQ14 E: 0.219969157 to 4 d.p. is 0.2200. The first 5 decimal places are 0.21996; the 6 is 'more than 5' so the 9 rounds up to a 10, this means that the next 9 has to be rounded to 10 and the 1 becomes 2.

NQ15 C: A 1200 m perimeter square field must have four equal sides of 300 m each. The area of the field is 300 m x 300 m = 90000 m^2.

NQ16 A: 170 ÷ 2.5 = 340 ÷ 5 = 680 ÷ 10 = 68 (doubling method).

NQ17 B: 10 pots = £7.50; 11 = £8.25; 12 = £9.00; 13 = £9.75

NQ18 C: $r(p - r)$ = 50(72-50) = 50 x 22 = 100 x 11 = 1100

NQ19 D: 1¾ ÷ 2½ = 3½ ÷ 5 = 7 ÷ 10 = 7/10 (doubling method).

NQ20 E: 1/60 x 360 = 360/60 = 6^0

NQ21 C: 1.33 (all numbers start 1.3; the smallest 2nd d.p. is 3 again).

NQ22 D: 40000x6.25 = 400x625 = 100x4x625 = 100x2500 = 250000

NQ23 E: 10% of £50 = £5; then 20% in coins = £10 and 80% in notes = £40 which is eight £5 notes.

NQ24 D: 87.5% is 87.5 ÷ 100 = 0.875 = 0.9 to 1 d.p.

NQ25 A: 44 = 8 x x or 8x = 44, then x = 44/8 = 5½

NQ26 B: 45 x 8/9 = 45 x 8 ÷ 9 = (45 ÷ 9) x 8 = 5 x 8 = 40

NQ27 D: factors of 88: 1,2,4,11,22,<u>44</u>, 88; factors of 44:1,2,4,11,<u>44</u>

NQ28 B: 80% = 80/100 = 8/10 = 4/5

NQ29 E: 2 pm to 10 pm = 8 hours; 8/12 = 2/3; 2/3 x 360^0 = 240^0

NQ30 A: 10.00 to 10.20 = 20/60 = 1/3; 1/3 x 360^0 = 120^0

EXPANDED ANSWERS: TEST 4

MQ1 C: 9 V across the bulb if 3 V across the resistor (9+3 = 12).

MQ2 A: Weight near to the fulcrum with the longest lever arm.

MQ3 A: Moving the fulcrum to the left is the only way to increase the leverage of the larger, though lighter weight.

MQ4 B: Compare mechanical advantages (MA's): A = 4; B = 5; C = 2

MQ5 D: Gear1/Gear2 = 12 teeth/8 teeth = 1.5; if Gear1 rotates at 1 rev/10 sec = 6 revs/min then Gear2 rotates at 6 x 1.5 = 9 rev/min.

MQ6 B: The top gear rotates ACW; the bottom gear rotates CW at twice the speed; the bottom rail moves to the left twice the speed.

MQ7 C: Four switches; 3 bulb switches and the battery switch.

MQ8 D: A variable resistor (variable as shown by the arrow).

MQ9 B: A high centre of mass (or gravity) displaced to the right.

MQ10 B: W x 4 (graduations) = 10x2 + 5x4 = 40; 4W = 40, so W=10.

MQ11 B: Car 'A' is steeper but stable because the centre of gravity (mass) is inside the lower wheels contact point; in Car B it is outside.

MQ12 C: This flywheel has more of its weight nearer the rim and will take longer to slow down (most angular momentum); B stops soonest.

MQ13 C: This fan has the largest diameter and the highest tip speed (the larger the diameter the more distance is traveled per revolution).

MQ14 C: This block is the heaviest (but not the most dense) because it displaces the greatest vol. of water (block wt = wt of water displaced).

MQ15 A: All the bulbs light (each has a pos/neg supply); 2 brightest.

MQ16 A: Depicts a fuse wire.

MQ17 D: David: 79 kg; Alan (75 kg) can only balance the weight.

MQ18 D: The bulbs share the voltage (3 volts each) and do not light.

MQ19 A: L1 and L2 share 12 volts (6 volts each) and will light.

MQ20 A: Mechanical advantage (MA) = 1; (B is 2, C is 3 and D is 2).

MQ21 A: 1 and 2 are clockwise, but not 4 as belt crosses over (so not 3 either) 6 is clockwise (belt crosses back) and 5 also; so 1,2,5 and 6.

MQ22 C: Mechanical advantage (MA) = 2; spring balance reads 2 kg and must be lifting 2 kg x MA = 4 kg, hence W = 3 kg.

MQ23 B: Greatest height difference between tank level and outlet.

MQ24 D: Acceleration due to gravity is the same whatever the mass.

MQ25 C: C2 topples; C3 can roll freely; C1 is stable on its base.

MQ26 A: The bottom bulb and the middle bulb complete the circuit.

MQ27 C: Lowest jar = greatest 'head' (despite having to climb higher).

MQ28 D: Into the wind (a south-westerly blows *from* the south-west).

MQ29 B: The weight on the right will drop.

MQ30 B: The waterline is highest on the hull (ship floats the lowest).

Printed in Great Britain
by Amazon

10599755R00115